Presidential
PASSAGES

Presidential PASSAGES
BY ROBERT F. CARBONE

FORMER COLLEGE PRESIDENTS REFLECT ON
THE SPLENDOR AND AGONY OF THEIR CAREERS

American Council on Education
Washington, D.C.

© 1981 by American Council on Education
One Dupont Circle, Washington, D.C. 20036

Library of Congress Cataloging in Publication Data
Carbone, Robert F., 1929–
  Presidential passages.

  Bibliography: p.
  1. College presidents—United States. I. Title.
LB2341.C163   378'.111   81-12823
ISBN 0-8268-1454-9   AACR2

9 8 7 6 5 4 3 2 1

Printed in the United States of America

To my parents, for giving me life and teaching me its value

To Richard and Catherine Henderson, for their help and encouragement along the way

To my wife, Suzanne, and my children, Angela and Christopher, for adding to my life the most important things of all

I would not have missed being a college president. I'd never try it again. I look back on it all and say I would not have missed it, but sometimes I wonder if it was worth all the buffeting, the endless hours, the fatigue, the days and nights away from the family, the cheap shots.
Retired president of a small college

Contents

Foreword *xi*

Preface—*The Presidency as Splendid Agony* *xv*

Acknowledgments *xvii*

PART I: ACADEMIC EXECUTIVES *1*

Chapter One—*A Generation of Former Presidents* *5*
Highest Degree Earned, Most Recent Position, Field of Academic Study, Length of Service, Age When Leaving Office, Other Interesting Facts about Presidents, Concluding Note

Chapter Two—*Former Presidents by Type of Institution* *16*
Community and Junior Colleges, State Colleges and Universities, State Universities and Land-Grant Colleges, Independent Colleges and Universities

PART II: AFTER THE PRESIDENCY *31*

Chapter Three—*Just Another Member of the Faculty: Returning to the Classroom* *33*
Why Return to Teaching?, Problems for Returning Teachers, Satisfaction in the Classroom

Chapter Four—*Back into the Fray: Taking Another Administrative Position in Higher Education* *39*
Positions on the Fringe, Other Campus Positions, Getting Promoted, From One Presidency to Another

Chapter Five—*Into the Real World: Moving to Industry, Government, or the Nonprofit Sector*   50
Nonacademic Opportunities, Why Leave Academe?, Comparing the Presidency with Other Jobs, Returning to the Presidency

Chapter Six—*Getting the Gold Watch: Retirement and Semiretirement*   59
Planning for Retirement, Where Presidents Retire, Retirement Activities, Adjustment to Retirement, Recalling the Highlights

PART III: LEARNING FROM THE PAST   67

Chapter Seven—*Straight from the Shoulder: Advice from Former College and University Presidents*   69
Entertaining Thoughts about a Presidency, Finding Someone to Help, Preparing for the Job, Voicing Presidential Aspirations, General Words of Advice

Chapter Eight—*Illusions about Presidential Leadership*   78
Myths and Realities about Presidents and the Presidency

Postscript—*Splendid Agony Revisited*   87

Suggestions for Further Reading   89

Foreword

Many books have been written by and about college and university presidents. Moreover, these same individuals are featured in the numerous histories of our institutions of higher education—quite a few of these histories read like chronicles of presidents rather than accounts of the development of the colleges and universities concerned. Then, too, there are volumes about the institution of the presidency, and still more material about the office in books discussing all or part of postsecondary education.

Here is plenty of reading. Do we need more?

Yes, we certainly do. For almost everything we have is out of date, obsolete, or at least obsolescent. The literature has historical value, of course, and that is not to be ignored (not by me, anyway, since my academic union card is in history). But much of what has been written on the presidency has little application to the present.

To be specific: higher education has gone through many revolutions in the decades since World War II—an enrollment revolution, a research revolution, an adult education revolution, an international education revolution, a student protest revolution, a service-to-society revolution, a revolution of rising expectations on the part of those left behind in earlier years. Inevitably, the presidency has been influenced by these developments. If anything, it has changed more than the institutions with which it is connected.

With the new selection processes, it takes forever to appoint a new president; yet the individual named may serve only a short time. With a handful of exceptions, such as Father Hesburgh at Notre Dame and Bill Friday in North Carolina, the presidents-for-a-generation are no more. Instead, the half-life of an incumbency has dropped well below five years. Heads of public and private institutions, of universities, colleges, and community colleges get worn out in service, or are eased out or dropped at an alarming rate. Meantime, there is talk that the job has become impossible, what with the problems of size and declining public and governmental support, not to mention the incredible complications stemming from affirmative action, court cases, environmental conflicts, inflation, shifting sex standards, and unionization.

In spite of all this, and in part because of it, the presidency remains important in higher education. Presidents make decisions on policy and management. They are involved in short-term and long-term action, in firefighting, and in redefining institutional goals. Their leadership, or lack of it, is a critical factor in the life of the colleges and universities they serve.

This means that there is a genuine need for studies of the presidency of postsecondary institutions as it has developed in recent years and is developing right now. How does the president of an enormous multicampus university or university system relate to his or her faculty, students, and staff? With all the crises of our era, how much time does a president have to think about the larger questions, such as the relationship of education to society? Has government support—and interference—changed the president's options? Are the chief officers of our community colleges and our urban institutions a different breed? How can men and women from academic backgrounds (*i.e.*, most presidents) hope to solve the giant fiscal and other problems facing higher education today? Are there any education statesmen in presidential posts anymore? (Try and name one.)

Fortunately, we are beginning to see some studies that describe and analyze various aspects of the contemporary presidency. One of my favorites is Joseph F. Kauffman's *At the Pleasure of the Board*, published in 1980 by the American Council on Education (which, as we know, is a sort of presidents' association and is to be congratulated for having run courses to help new members of the fraternity get ready for the burdens that will soon descend upon them). Kauffman's carefully prepared book shows how times have changed presidential searches and the roles and tenure of chief executives. Himself a former president as well as a student of the subject, he knows the horrors associated with the college and university presidency but manages to finish on the upbeat.

The present volume takes up where Kauffman's leaves off, examining the experiences and present situation of expresidents. It also ends on an optimistic note, even though many of those cooperating in the study ended their presidential terms on sour notes.

This book has a special interest for me, for I belong to the company of those who were presidents and do not now have that title. And, like most others in that category, I look back on the presidential years as the most important part of my career.

I am also interested because the author got his first major taste of administration in higher education as a member of my University of Wisconsin staff. That, however, is only one part of Bob Carbone's background. As a teacher-scholar-administrator with experience all the way from elementary to postgraduate levels, he has all the proper credentials to undertake an investigation such as this.

Instead of focusing on one type of institution—say, the major universities or the prestigious private colleges—Dr. Carbone has taken on the whole sweep of American colleges and universities. His queries have brought good responses, perhaps because those who have left the job of president have more time to answer questions than when they were on the firing line. (And the replies are their own, whereas many sitting presidents use ghost writers for questionnaires as well as for speeches.)

The picture that emerges is of an assorted but talented batch of individuals who found both pleasure and pain—*splendid agony*—in their years of service as presidents. Most of them served in the challenging and sometimes terrifying era of expansion and protest, a period now followed by one of financial crisis and discouragement. Generally, they look back on their days in high office with more satisfaction than sorrow. Happily, nearly all have been able to do useful things in and outside academe in their postpresidential years. That is, they have not found it necessary to spend much of their time boasting about their presidential achievements and explaining away their blunders. Looking back, they have interesting, even wise, things to say about the role of the college or university president, and they gently offer good advice that their successors probably should and probably will not follow.

All together, I am pleased to see a book based on the careers and thoughts of our band of former presidents, and am further pleased that it is a competent study of value to those who are interested in higher education. (And who is not, even in these dismal days?)

FRED HARVEY HARRINGTON

Preface: The Presidency as "Splendid Agony"

In speaking of his years as head of an American college, one former president described the presidency as "splendid agony." Many comments of former college and university presidents that appear in this book clearly illustrate his point.

Reports of presidential life, such as those by a generation of former college and university presidents included in this book, portray the conflicting qualities of this important position. On one hand, the excitement and satisfaction of leadership create a kind of splendor few mortals can resist. On the other hand, presidents are the vortex of a human enterprise that demands of them decisions that are routinely difficult and often agonizing. I sought to capture this discordant nature of the college and university presidency in this book.

Much of what has been written about the presidency was produced by former presidents. At one time, perhaps, there was little else for retired presidents to do but write about their experiences. Publishing a book or article was just the ticket for one whose scholarly skills may have suffered from long years of working on the budget. Besides, writing was an enjoyable and therapeutic way of exorcising all those feelings one could not express while encumbered with the responsibilities of office.

Presidential ego must also have motivated many of the writers. The job of president undoubtedly requires a certain strength of mind and will that does not automatically atrophy when a president goes back to teaching or gives up the all-day trustees' meeting for a gentle afternoon staking the tomatoes. One former president put it this way:

> *Most refugees from the ivory tower find themselves fascinating topics, like bar bums who repeat their stories about the day they stormed ashore at Idaho beachhead.*

More likely, all this commentary about the presidency and about the people who carry that title probably exists because the presidency is important. It's the top of the line, regardless of what chronically cynical academics say. "[It was] the most exciting, demanding, and satisfying experience of my life," said a recently retired president. Who can dispute that testimony?

Although much of what has been written about presidents flows from their own pens, the subject has also interested many students of higher education administration. In addition, the presidency draws the attention of higher education associations. The American Council on Education and the Association of Governing Boards, for example, have produced valuable contributions to the literature. The topic has also inspired academics who always wanted to be president but who never got the nod—as if, by vicariously grasping the mace for a time, they can lay aside thoughts of presidential authority and settle for a cushy professorship somewhere.

Given all this prose on the presidency, why yet another book for presidents (serving, aspiring, or retired) and for president watchers? A retrospective view of the presidency is needed, one based on insights from an entire generation of those who sat at presidential desks. The question I asked was, What happens after the presidency? The pages that follow offer some answers to that question.

There was yet another reason for examining this difficult but rewarding job and for questioning the people who enjoyed(?) it. Having a keen interest in career mobility and in midcareer change, I wondered how college presidents manage their careers, how they prepare for retirement, and how they fare after leaving office.

As our population ages, concern about midcareer change and creative retirement increases. Hence, it appeared useful to examine how these phenomena operate in higher education, especially regarding presidents of colleges and universities. What emerged was a glimpse of how higher education treats its executive officers after they are selected and what happens to them after they have given a portion of their lives to institutional leadership.

This book provides some insight into how higher education and society in general benefit from the experience and talent of those who were college and university presidents. By examining the "splendid agony" of presidential life, this book may help readers decide whether the benefits offered by this important office outweigh the burdens.

Acknowledgments

The opportunity to work for two outstanding university presidents early in my career undoubtedly sparked my interest in the college and university presidency. My debt to them is great.

In 1961, fresh out of graduate school, I joined a small staff gathered together by James Bryant Conant, who was then beginning his critical study of teacher education in America. For twenty years, Mr. Conant served as president of Harvard. Nearly a decade before I joined his staff, he left Harvard to become High Commissioner and then Ambassador to the Federal Republic of Germany. Accounts of his presidential days, as well as those of his work as diplomat and education reformer, gave me a magnificent introduction to the "several lives" that college and university presidents often lead. The lessons Mr. Conant taught me, by word and deed, have forever marked my life, for which I am deeply grateful.

The second university president with whom I was associated was Fred Harvey Harrington, the president of the University of Wisconsin. For five years in the turbulent 1960s I had almost daily contact with Mr. Harrington, first as an intern in the office of his vice president, and later as his special assistant. Those glorious but stressful days afforded me an opportunity to observe decisive, creative presidential leadership under the most adverse conditions. After leaving the presidency, Mr. Harrington continued his career as a Ford Foundation officer in India, as author of a useful book on adult education, and as teacher-scholar in history. The foreword of this book is just the latest example of his continued contribution to my education.

Of course, there were many others who, knowingly or unknowingly, fostered the growth of this book. Charles Fisher of the American Council on Education was enthusiastic about a study of former presidents and encouraged me to do it. A small grant from the Bureau of Educational Research and Field Services in the College of Education, University of Maryland, covered printing of the questionnaires and postage for follow-up correspondence. Thanks are due four persons and the education associations they represent for distributing more than three thousand inquiries that yielded basic data on former college and university presidents. They are Garvin Hudgins, National Association of State Universities and Land-Grant Colleges; Virginia Fadil, National Institute of Independent Colleges and Universities; Roger Yarrington, American Association of Community and Junior Colleges; and Allan Ostar, American Association of State Colleges and Universities.

Preparations for this book included a graduate seminar on the college and university presidency that I offered in spring 1980. Several seminar sessions featured guests who were well qualified to discuss the presidency and those who serve in that position. These guests were Malcolm Moos, former president of the University of Minnesota; Deborah Toll, whose husband is president of the University of Maryland; Raphael Cortada, president of the Community College of Baltimore; John Nason, former president of Carleton College; and Nancy Axelrod, vice president for programs and public policy, Association of Governing Boards. Each contributed in some way to my understanding of the presidency, and to each go my thanks.

I would also like to thank the graduate students who participated in the seminar, especially those who permitted me to use some of the information they collected. Members of the latter group are identified at appropriate places in the book. My final thanks go to Michael Nofi, another graduate student in higher education administration, who did a superb job of compiling sources.

PART I
ACADEMIC EXECUTIVES

In all honesty, I do not know how to rate my college presidency vis à vis my other jobs. It was too unique, like getting married, or holding your firstborn child. There is nothing like it.
Former president of a liberal arts college

There are more than three thousand colleges and universities in the United States, and each one has a president. Of course, not every institution of higher education calls its chief administrative officer "president." However, that is the most common title used. Therefore, in this book, the term president will include all the alternative titles—chancellor, provost, or any others that may exist.

Hardly anyone calls college and university presidents "academic executives," yet that is exactly what they are. Long gone is the day, if it ever existed, when presidents were the intellectual leaders on campus. In recent decades their work has been managerial rather than scholarly.

Thorstein Veblen was among the first to notice this shift. He called presidents "captains of erudition" and likened them to the robber barons who steered the ships of business and industry. Of course, Veblen didn't like trustees either, and he advocated wiping out both presidents and board members. (If Veblen meant to suggest that the faculty could manage affairs in a modern college or university, then faculty meetings of his day could not have resembled their contemporary counterparts.)

Although modern presidents hear few cries for doing away with their positions, some members of the academic community still do not hold them in high regard. Rarely do presidents enjoy the wholehearted support of faculty members. Maybe the cynicism comes from professors who like to exercise the critical skills they learned as graduate students. Maybe professors really are "people who think otherwise." Whatever the reason, the feeling is captured in this squib, offered by a man who had worked closely with many presidents:

I remember one state university president staring contemplatively out his window at a swarm of faculty coming out of an adjacent building following a general faculty meeting. "Look," he said, "there go a couple thousand people who are convinced that they know more about how to run this university than I do."

Regardless of whether faculty wisdom is correct on that score, presidents in American institutions are in difficult, demanding, and vital positions. The American college presidency has evolved into a much more complex job than its European counterpart. Both ceremonial functions of *rektor* and managerial responsibilities of *vice rektor* accrue to American presidents.

The office of president presents both rewards and burdens. As this study reveals, presidents who look back on their terms of office often lament the demands on their time, pressures on their families, barbs of their critics, and the difficulty of having to make decisions in an institution where power is shared and loyalties divided. Yet former presidents also admit that they found presidential duties rewarding. Many enjoyed the feeling of power, the sense of authority, the challenge of leadership. If they were weary, their fatigue resulted from being engaged in important work. If they were frustrated, their anxiety came from attacking problems that were neither trivial nor easily solved. One former president summed it up in these words: "The college presidency is somewhat like self-flagellation: it hurts, but it feels so nice."

Enough has been written about college and university presidents to guarantee consensus about the nature of their duties. Considerable attention has focused on presidential selection, and several reports have addressed presidential evaluation. However, this book shares only one characteristic with earlier reports on the topic—it begins with demographic data on a generation of college and university presidents—those who recently cleaned out their desks and who moved on to other things. Following these data is a discussion of their midcareer changes and postcareer activities.

PART I: ACADEMIC EXECUTIVES

ONE

A Generation of Former Presidents

The only difficulty of leaving the presidency was the initial shock. People who had seemingly been my best friends for years now did not even say hello to me. I thought maybe I was a criminal or something of the sort. Hundreds of people who formerly were most cooperative suddenly dropped me like a hot potato. But, of course, it's very good to be rid of such phony "friends." No doubt they "boot lick" the new president—and maybe he believes them, too.
Small college president who retired

When students begin their trek back to campus each fall, there is someone—a president or acting president—making plans to guide that institution through the year ahead. There is also a generation of academicians who once guided those institutions and who have now gone on to other things.

This book describes that cohort of academicians who, in fall 1979, were the immediate past presidents of American colleges and universities. Data gathered on 1,406 previous inhabitants of presidential suites provides a comprehensive profile of this generation of former college and university presidents.

When secretaries or assistants in presidential offices around the academic circuit open the morning mail, they almost always find at least one letter, accompanied by a questionnaire, asking for information about the institution. Such inquiries are usually bucked down to institutional research, where they get placed on the stack and—sometimes—even elicit responses. The questionnaire that yielded data for this analysis motivated just under half of the recipients to respond.

The study sample—one of every two former presidents in the fall 1979 cohort—reveals interesting facts about those selected to lead colleges and universities.

We have no forwarding address for President X. There is nothing in the file that gives much about his professional background. I've heard, and cannot confirm the information, that he had a doctorate in education from Y or Z. He served as president here eight years and my information, again unconfirmed, is that he took a medical disability retirement, based largely on a history of ulcers.
Letter from a state college president regarding his predecessor

---

Highest Degree Earned

Among all academic degrees, the Ph.D., especially in one of the traditional liberal arts disciplines, is considered the most prestigious. Whether that unofficial ranking is justified or not, conventional wisdom suggests that few if any college presidents should be without one. Conventional wisdom, however, is wrong in this instance. Just under half, or 679 (48 percent), of the former presidents surveyed had Ph.D.'s.

Of course, a higher percentage held doctorates of some sort. Actually, 67 percent of the former presidents could be addressed by the title "doctor." A total of 197 (14 percent) had Ed.D.'s, 45 (3 percent) earned doctorates in theology, 20 (1 percent) had doctorates in legal studies, and another 19 (1 percent) held other types of doctorates.

The highest degree awarded to 260 former presidents (19 percent) was a Master of Arts or a Master of Science. Most surprising of all, however, was the fact that 69 (5 percent) had only bachelor's degrees.

(No information about academic degrees was provided on 117, or 8 percent, of the group studied.)

These data reveal one reality about the selection of presidents for American colleges and universities: it isn't always the candidate's academic credentials that yield the prize. When search committees and governing boards decide who is to head an institution of higher education, certain factors in selection override the importance of a Ph.D. or any other doctoral degree. One factor is the prior experience of the candidate. As the following data indicate, most of the former presidents described had paid their dues in the academic enterprise by serving in subordinate academic positions. However, a surprisingly large number of presidents did not move up the academic ladder at all: instead, they came from outside academe and climbed over the ivy walls, as the following section reveals.

A chief administrator of a college or university must first have been successful as a faculty member, as a classroom teacher, and as an active participant in an effective form of faculty governance.
Former president who now teaches

Most Recent Position

If a random sample of academics were asked about stepping stones to the presidency, a frequent response would probably be "the vice presidency or deanship." But that answer is more wrong than right.

The single largest group among the 1,406 former presidents covered in this study was not even on campus just prior to assuming the presidency. Three hundred eleven of them (22 percent) held positions outside postsecondary education. Of that number, more than a third were members of some religious order, and the remainder held positions ranging from military officer to archivist, from school superintendent to government official, from museum director to state judge.

Moving to the presidency from a nonacademic position is the mode only when all institutions of higher education are considered as a group. The trend undoubtedly reflects the large number of church-related colleges and universities in the private sector. When public institutions are considered separately, the more conventional route to the presidency is much more prevalent. (Details of previous positions held by presidents in each type of institution will be presented in the next chapter.)

Among academic positions, the deanship appears to be the best spot on campus for those who seek access to the presidency. Twenty-one percent of the former presidents surveyed were deans immediately prior to their presidency, and only 12 percent were vice presidents. No distinction was made in this analysis among the portfolios the deans carried; thus, the category includes deans of students and chapels as well as deans of academic or professional schools. The vice presidential category also included the full range of titles associated with this position.

Moving from one presidency to another was not a particularly popular step, for only 155 (11 percent) of these former presidents did so. There appeared to be proportionately more community college presidents in this category than presidents from four-year colleges and universities. Close behind, in terms of previous position held, were the professors. A somewhat surprising 147 (10 percent) of the

---

The avenues to a college or university presidency are, I am sure, many and varied. My leanings, colored by my own experience, favor the person who has gone up through the academic ranks in some specific subject matter area. In that manner, he will develop a feel for the whole enterprise and will have some special understanding and knowledge of one key area, namely, the academic.
Retired president of a private college

If someone is preparing for a president's position, I believe that the best background would be graduate study in administration and planning.
Emeritus president

presidents surveyed moved directly from the classroom to the president's office. Again, this was more common in the private institutions than in the public ones. Only 49 (3 percent) of the total sample moved from the position of department chairman to the top spot on campus, and 88 (6 percent) previously held some other academic position. Included in this latter group were provosts, business managers, presidential assistants, development officers, and even one coach.

Chapter 2, with separate sections on each type of institution, offers a more detailed and more in-depth discussion of these data. It will suffice to conclude here that more presidents come from outside academe than is generally suspected and that there are various routes inside the institutions to becoming president.

Field of Academic Study

Another view of the academic executives can be gained by examining the fields in which they earned their highest academic degrees. The largest contingent of presidents in this cohort, 375 (27 percent) earned their highest degrees in education. Nearly half the community college presidents and a quarter of the state college presidents did their academic work in schools of education.

Studies in the humanities yielded the highest degrees for the next largest group of former presidents—249 (19 percent). The large number of church-related colleges and universities in this country reflects the large number of former presidents (212, or 15 percent) who earned their highest degrees in philosophy, theology, or religion. Next were the social sciences, in which 164 (12 percent) of those surveyed held their final degrees.

Fewer than one in ten of the former presidents earned final degrees in physical sciences or mathematics. The fields of business administration, law, engineering, and the biological sciences involved less than 5 percent while medicine and foreign languages each accounted for fewer than 1 percent. Information on the academic fields of 130 (9 percent) of the former presidents included in this survey was not provided by the institutions they had served.

Length of Service

Whenever table talk at the faculty dining room turns to the vagaries of presidential activity, one topic that usually emerges is how long (or short) a term the president will serve. Because most veteran professors have seen presidents come and go, conventional wisdom on campus insists that presidential terms are short and growing shorter. That rule of thumb, however, is a rather rough estimate of reality.

To be sure, the day of exceedingly long presidential terms may be over. No president in the generation of academic executives being described here came close to matching the term of America's all-time record holder as head of an academic institution: in the nineteenth century, Eliphalet Nott served as president of Union College in Schenectady "for the incredible term of sixty-two years."[1] The 44-year stewardship of Nicholas Murray Butler at Columbia University is another example of the length presidential terms used to be.

I do not think any president should stay more than ten years. Move to another campus if you are young enough, or take on a teaching job as part of your contractual obligation. You've given your best in that time, and there is little juice left in the lemon.
Retired president of a private junior college

I have found that the presidency (seventeen years) effectively eliminated my professional career and, in retrospect, I would not do it again.
Former state college president

It is a sad commentary on the academic condition that many recent presidents hardly got their books unpacked before finding it expedient (or necessary) to move on. One-fourth of all presidents in the survey served only one to four years. It is shocking that of the 345 short-term presidents, twenty-four were in office only a single year. Perhaps some of them were acting or interim presidents. These data suggest, however, that despite elaborate and expensive procedures for selecting new presidents, American colleges and universities frequently come up with mismatches. Of course, a short stint in office does not always mean that the president walked into a meat grinder. Some

1. J. S. Brubacher and W. Rudy, *Higher Education in Transition* (New York: Harper, 1958), p. 100.

short-term presidents accepted presidencies in larger or more prestigious institutions, and others moved up to systemwide positions. In such cases, selection procedures may have worked too well, attracting a leader whose talents exceeded the local challenge.

The vast majority of presidents, however, remained in office long enough to leave a mark on the institution. Nearly 500 presidents (35 percent) in the sample served from five to ten years, and just under 260 other presidents (18 percent) held the office from eleven to nineteen years. Eight percent, or 111, headed their institutions for more than thirty years. Information on length of service was lacking for 196 (14 percent) of the responding presidents.

None of the more than 1,400 presidents included in this report could claim longevity in office equal to that of Nott or even to Butler, but some came close. Among the presidents who served more than twenty years, the most senior in service spent forty-one years as president of a small church-related institution. A public university president headed his institution for forty years, and a score of presidents in both the public and private sectors served from twenty to thirty-nine years.

Because rapid turnover in the office of president is considered detrimental to institutional welfare, the demographic characteristics of long-term presidents were given some special analysis. Unfortunately, the analysis yielded little that could be used as a predictor of durability in office.

As might be expected, the highest percentage of veteran presidents retired when leaving office although many continued active professional lives even after completing twenty or more years in office. Some returned to teaching, but three times as many moved to some other administrative post in academe, and four times as many found interesting things to do outside academe.

The profile of veteran presidents is not markedly different from that of all presidents in terms of highest degree earned or field of academic specialization. Position held just prior to becoming president, however, provides one distinction. About one in five had been professors, and an equal proportion had been deans. Fewer had previously served as presidents of other institutions or as vice presidents, and a surprisingly large number of long-term presidents came from nonacademic positions. Many of the latter group were clergy who assumed presidencies in church-related institutions, but three

> *The president seldom has time to take stock of how well or how badly he is doing until he bails out or runs screaming for the horizon or achieves the inner peace of complete breakdown.*
> Former president who returned to administration

were state school superintendents and five were local school superintendents. The list also includes an archivist, an engineer, a private school headmaster, a coach, a development officer, and a U.S. State Department employee.

Age When Leaving Office

Further insight into the lives of these college and university presidents is revealed by the ages at which they left office. Of the 1,406 presidents surveyed, 159 (11 percent) left at age sixty-five, but an even larger number—179 (13 percent)—stayed in office for one or more years beyond age sixty-five. The former were mostly from public institutions, many of which have policies that require administrators to hand over the keys when they reach conventional retirement age. On the other hand, independent institutions rarely have such rules; hence, they are more heavily represented in the group of presidents who continued in office after age sixty-five.

Nearly half of all former presidents made some kind of career move between the ages of fifty and sixty-four. For many, the move was to another academic position—generally, another presidency. Others abandoned the academic scene completely, taking a variety of positions that will be described in more detail in a later chapter.

There was also considerable career mobility among the youngest subset of presidents: those 278 presidents (20 percent) who were forty-nine years of age and younger. As might be expected, a larger proportion of these presidents remained in the academic world and continued their leadership roles by assuming presidencies in other colleges and universities. Still, some seemed to find the presidency more than they bargained for and returned to the classroom or left the academic environment entirely. More will be said about their new positions in subsequent chapters.

Other Interesting Facts about Presidents

Any study of this nature will turn up some interesting and unexpected bits of information. The incidental facts reported below are offered to help round out this glimpse of a generation of college and university presidents. The first fact concerns those presidents who headed institutions that had no former president because the so-called founding president is still in office. Secondly, and less happily, some data were collected on mortality rates among college and university presidents.

A considerable number of presidents can claim the distinction of being the only chief executive their college or university has ever had. Forty-four institutions (3 percent) said their founding president was still serving. Most of these institutions were community colleges, as might be expected, considering the dramatic growth in the number of community colleges in the 1960s and 1970s. The twenty-eight founding presidents of community colleges constitute one-tenth of community college presidents covered by the survey. If that group is representative of all community college presidents, then there are probably about one hundred community college presidents in this country who still administer the institutions they helped to establish.

I was privileged to work closely with a number of strong and accomplished university presidents all my professional life, so I was aware of all the warts and moles and blemishes of the office at a rather tender age.
Former private college president

Among state colleges, ten founding presidents emerged from a total of 231 presidents identified in the study. That figure appears surprisingly high because many of these institutions, once normal schools and teachers' colleges, have been operating for several generations. Yet several opened during higher education's boom years and, in some at least, founding presidents continue to serve. None of the major public universities, the vast majority of which came into being in the nineteenth century or earlier, reported a founding president in office. Finally, six independent colleges in the sample were still administered by founding presidents. This reflects the penchant for some philanthropists to support the establishment of new private institutions even though financial and enrollment problems force dozens of them to merge or close their doors.

In light of all the pressures on college and university presidents, it is understandable that some of them suffer health problems or even die while in office. Nearly sixty of the more than 1,400 presidents did not have the opportunity to explore new career ventures—they died before their terms of office ended. The mortality rate was 2 percent for both state college and major public university presidents, 4 percent for community college presidents, and as high as 5 percent for independent college and university presidents. These differing rates are puzzling because the factors of mortality and length of time in office seem to be independent of each other.

The presidency involves administrative skills, and these are more than logic alone. There is logic involved, but you do not manage a large, intelligent group of people by logic alone. Administration is a skill.
Former state university president

Concluding Note

This initial look at former college and university presidents generally groups them without regard for the types of institutions they headed. However informative, such a general overview obscures many of the more interesting facets of presidential life that distinguish the various segments of American higher education. Generalizations about phenomena in higher education are almost always more precise when they pertain to groups of similar institutions. The next chapter devotes a section to each of four subsets of the 1,406 institutions surveyed.

There are many ways to categorize institutions of higher education. In this book, the breakdown is by what is often called control. Public colleges and universities, whose boards are appointed by government or elected by citizens, constitute one major type of institution. This category is divided into three more homogeneous groups: community and junior colleges, state colleges, and state universities.

Another major category of institutions is the so-called independent or private college or university, which does not have a board appointed by governmental officials or elected by citizens. Control of colleges and universities in this category generally resides in self-perpetuating boards of trustees or, in some cases, religious orders. No attempt has been made to distinguish between nonsectarian institutions and those with religious affiliations. Because there are dramatic differences in enrollments among various independent institutions, however, certain facts associated with institutional size are reported.

PART I: ACADEMIC EXECUTIVES

TWO

Former Presidents by Type of Institution

It is impossible for a board of trustees and a president to know how it is all going to work out until the marriage takes place and some time has been spent living together. If both parties ever knew everything about each other, they would never be able to get together.
A president in his second presidency

Thus far, I have described a generation of former college and university presidents in general terms, ignoring the important fact that American higher education covers a spectrum of strikingly different institutions. The presidency often reflects the distinguishing characteristics of its institutions. Similarly, the people who hold this office may also reflect some of those distinctions.

The 1,406 colleges and universities included in this report were classified by the national associations to which they belonged. The 295 two-year institutions belonged to the American Association of Community and Junior Colleges (AACJC). The 231 general state colleges and universities were members of the American Association of State Colleges and Universities (AASCU). The 106 comprehensive public universities belonged to the National Association of State Universities and Land-Grant Colleges (NASULGC). Finally, the 774 private institutions held membership in the National Association of Independent Colleges and Universities (NAICU).

So facile a sorting method may appear completely arbitrary, but there is some logic involved. Individually, these four associations constitute the primary reference groups for the various types of American colleges and universities. Most presidents spend their entire professional careers teaching or administering in institutions that share similar characteristics: there is little movement from public to private or from two-year to four-year institutions. This analysis enables readers to develop a better understanding of the presidency—and of life after the presidency—within homogeneous groups of higher education institutions.

Readers interested in private liberal arts colleges may want to concentrate on the NAICU data, but doing only that deprives them of interesting insights into how presidents of those institutions differ from counterparts in the public sector. The same loss of perspective would be true for readers who concentrate solely on any other single type of institution.

After ten years, how much longer should I seek to maintain my presidency? Does my continued service help or hurt the college? If I should leave my job, which I love, then what should I do with the rest of my life?
A community college president in his second presidency

Community and Junior Colleges

Although nearly 1,100 community and junior colleges were surveyed in this study, only 295 institutions responded with information about the immediate past president. This suggests that readers should be cautious in generalizing the data to all community colleges. The modest response rate may reflect a general disinterest in research in community colleges or, more likely, uncertainty about the position of president in these institutions.

A surprisingly large number of community college presidents in the sample served extremely short terms—one, two, or three years. Worse yet, some of them left office under stressful conditions. Two community colleges reported that their former presidents were "unemployed," and another indicated that the activities of its former president were "not known." One president who had served as chief executive of a college for twelve years reportedly "hadn't found anything yet" nearly a year after leaving office. And another, whose "address is unknown," served as president a single year. His former college reported, "It is believed he took a job in Texas; he resigned under pressure from the board, was given ninety days separation pay."

Of course, most of the community college presidents surveyed found interesting and useful things to do after leaving office. Of the 295 included in this category, 10 percent of them returned to the classroom and resumed teaching. Nineteen percent assumed another presidency. Of these, most moved to another community college although three became university presidents, and one was named head of a foreign institution.

Because many community colleges are in multicampus systems, it is natural that some of their presidents move to system leadership positions. That was the case with 4 percent of the sample group. Ten percent moved to other positions in higher education. One president stepped down and then became executive assistant to his successor; another was named assistant to the system head. Two former presidents took over continuing education responsibilities, one returned to the dean of students post on his campus, another became the campus development officer, and yet another became deputy director of the state higher education planning commission. Nine percent of the group were founding presidents of their institutions and continued to serve in that office.

Nearly a quarter (22 percent) of the former community college presidents entered full retirement, and an additional 7 percent were semiretired at the time of the survey. Of the latter, many continued to contribute to their institutions. One became chairman of the board of trustees, several were retained as consultants to the board and the new president, and others taught part time or engaged in special projects for the college, such as heading a newly established college foundation. Still others became free-lance consultants. Four percent of these presidents died in office; another 2 percent passed away after leaving office.

Activities outside the academic world claimed the attention of 13 percent of these former community college presidents. Eight became full-time consultants, six entered business, four became school superintendents, one was appointed state superintendent of schools, three took over school administration posts, two engaged in religious work, one was elected to a state legislature, and one worked as a legislative aide. Others worked for the government, farmed, joined a foundation staff, wrote a college history, or started their own businesses.

The demographic profile of the sample cohort reveals that 33 percent of them held a doctorate in the field of education and 27 percent had doctoral degrees from other fields. For 23 percent, the highest earned degree was a master's, and two of the 295 presidents had only bachelor's degrees. Forty-nine percent majored in education, 12 percent in the humanities, and 5 percent each in the social sciences, physical sciences, and business. Smaller numbers of presidents came from engineering, the biological sciences, agriculture, languages, law, speech pathology, religion, and labor relations.

Just prior to becoming president, these individuals held a variety of academic and nonacademic positions. Twenty-three percent moved to the campus from outside postsecondary education. Of these, most had been school superintendents, state school officials, or teachers, and others came from the military, business, government, and the clergy. The previous position of 29 percent was dean or director on campus. Fourteen percent moved from other presidencies, 9 percent were vice presidents, 6 percent professors, 2 percent department heads, and 3 percent other academic positions.

The length of terms of service as president varied from one to thirty years. Twenty-nine percent of the cohort served short-term— six served only one year, twenty served two years, thirty-nine served three years, and twenty-two served four years. On the other hand, 31 percent served up to ten years, 27 percent served from ten to twenty years, and 5 percent served more than twenty years.

Data were also collected on the age when these presidents left office. Six percent remained in office beyond the age of sixty-five, while 9 percent left exactly at age sixty-five. Many apparently made midcareer transitions—44 percent changed jobs between ages fifty and sixty-four, and 5 percent left the presidency before reaching the age of forty years. It is assumed that many of the younger presidents moved to other presidencies or to positions as system heads, but a few left the community college field altogether, a fact that underlines the kind of pressures many institutional heads must endure.

State Colleges and Universities

More than four hundred publicly supported institutions in this country are four-year state colleges and universities. Most are oriented toward undergraduate education but offer graduate work through the master's degree. Some have doctoral programs and, consequently, place some emphasis on research. All consider public service an important responsibility. The data that follow were provided by 231 of those institutions.

In the presidency, you never finish anything. Every day, twenty-four hours a day, month after month, stuff goes on and on and on. You might think you have something finished, but years later some nut will drag it all up again. I'm seeing this happening now. Things we settled ten years ago are reappearing. History and the experience of history mean nothing. To someone it's all brand new and someone has to invent the wheel all over again.
Former state college president

Presidents who serve AASCU institutions generally find interesting things to do after leaving office, but a few encounter difficulties. One former president in this group was unemployed for a period of time, another reportedly was "undecided about future plans" when this survey was taken, and the activities of yet another were unknown by the administration that succeeded him.

Teaching beckoned 19 percent of these presidents back to the classroom, usually at the same institutions they served as chief executive. An equal proportion moved on to another presidency or to the top position in a higher education system. Another 15 percent assumed some lower-level position within the academic community: vice president, development officer, system staff assistant, state coordinating board member, or other campus officer.

The world outside academe presented opportunities for 15 percent of these AASCU executives. One was elected lieutenant governor of his state, another served in the state senate, four took executive positions in state government, and six entered federal service. Seven others moved to business or industry, two set up consulting firms, four became association executives, three engaged in religious work, two assumed school system administrative positions, one joined a foundation staff, and one became a farmer.

Five percent of these former presidents were semiretired. Among the activities they pursued were service as chairmen of city and state commissions, part-time teaching, fund raising, and consulting. Full retirement was the decision of another 20 percent of the presidents in this group.

Because some state colleges and universities are relatively young institutions, 4 percent of those surveyed were still administered by the founding president. Death claimed six AASCU presidents while they were still in office, and three others died between the time they left office and the time of the study—a mortality rate of about 4 percent.

Long service as president was not uncommon among these former state college and university executives. One served forty-one years, and others served thirty-nine, thirty-five, and thirty-four years. But there were also some short-timers. Nineteen percent of the group served from one to four years. One died during his first year in office, another served for one year, eleven served for two years, fourteen served three years, and eighteen moved on after four years in the presidency. Thirty-one percent reported service of from five to ten years, an additional 27 percent served eleven to twenty years, and 8 percent remained in office more than twenty years.

Their academic training was more extensive than that of community college presidents. Among the 231 AASCU executives, 59 percent had earned a Ph.D., 23 percent held Ed.D. degrees, and 3 percent had other doctorates, 8 percent held master's degrees, and 3 percent had only bachelor's degrees. The major fields of study for this group were education (36 percent), humanities (21 percent), social sciences (14 percent), physical sciences (7 percent), and approximately 3 percent each in the fields of engineering, law, agriculture, biological sciences, and business.

Seventeen percent of those described here had previously served as president of another institution, and an equal proportion moved up from a vice presidential spot. The deanship, however, was the stepping stone for 27 percent, who had previous service at that level. Only 4 percent were department chairmen just prior to being selected president, and 14 percent held some other academic position, including that of professor. Seven percent came from outside academe, including a diplomat, a dozen school superintendents, five government officials, two military officers, several business executives, an accrediting association officer, and a coach.

There was a good deal of midcareer movement among these academic executives. Although 8 percent remained in office past the age of sixty-five, and 9 percent left at age sixty-five, more than half of them (53 percent) left office between the ages of fifty and sixty-four. Another 18 percent left office between the ages of thirty-five and forty-nine, most moving to other academic positions, but, as was true for community college presidents, a few moved on to completely different sectors of society.

As chancellor, I most enjoyed the associations and relationships with a wide variety of people and problems. The chief comparison [with returning to teaching] is not of better or worse, but rather of poignancy regarding exercise of authority, of having to take responsibility for rich and value-laden human situations. Teachers face too little of that. For a president, that is the critical measure of leadership.
Former public university chancellor

State Universities and Land-Grant Colleges

When presidents of major state universities or land-grant colleges decide it is time for a change in life style, most of them continue their administrative careers elsewhere. At least that is what the data on former presidents from 106 NASULGC institutions suggest. Because there are about 130 such institutions, the response rate was very high in this case, and the picture these data present is more complete. As might be expected, some NASULGC presidents face uncertain futures, too. One former president was "undecided" about next steps when this survey was taken, and another had "not yet determined" what he would do.

The 20 percent of NASULGC presidents who returned to teaching appeared to have two classroom options. Most taught in their original fields of academic training, but some shared their presidential experience and knowledge with graduate students in higher education administration. Another presidency or system executive's position claimed an additional 19 percent of these groups; in most cases, they moved to other NASULGC institutions or systems. Some, however, left the public sector for presidencies in independent institutions, including two major private research universities.

One-quarter of the former NASULGC presidents moved to responsible positions outside academe. Included in these positions were state cabinet secretary, commissioner of the U.S. Office of Education, assistant to the president of the United States, ambassador, director of AID, and administrator of NASA. Other former public university presidents became heads of associations, foundations, research institutes and centers, international projects, consulting firms, Radio Free Europe, and the Corporation for Public Broadcasting. Several others took positions in business and industry, one became a superintendent of schools, and one returned to the ministry.

Only 12 percent of the NASULGC presidents entered full retirement, and an additional 6 percent became semiretired. This latter group served on corporate boards, in fund raising, consulting, or part-time teaching. Two died in office, and five others passed away after leaving office.

The vast majority of these presidents had earned doctorates: 67 percent of them had Ph.D.'s and 5 percent Ed.D.'s. Fourteen percent attained the presidency with only a master's degree, and 4 percent achieved that status without having earned a graduate degree at all. The social sciences produced 21 percent of these university executives, while 16 percent did their work in the field of education, 14 percent in physical science and mathematics, 11 percent in humanities (including history), 9 percent in agriculture, 7 percent in law, 4 percent in engineering, 3 percent in biological sciences, 2 percent in business administration, 1 percent from foreign languages, and an additional 8 percent from all other academic fields.

Not surprisingly, nine out of ten NASULGC presidents moved up from within the academic enterprise. Nineteen percent had previous service as a president, 32 percent had served as vice presidents, and 23 percent were deans or directors. Another 9 percent held other academic positions: two were professors, three were presidential assistants, one was a department chairman, and four were in other campus jobs. The 10 percent who came from outside academe included one diplomat, four government officials, two foundation executives, and three businessmen.

Most NASULGC presidents served between five and twenty years in that office, but one served thirty years, and another was in office only one year. More specifically, 23 percent of them served four years or less. (Nine served two years, four served three years, and ten served four years.) Thirty-eight percent were in office from five to ten years, and 34 percent served between ten and twenty years. More than twenty years of service were recorded by about 5 percent of these presidents.

There was not enough time to think, to plan, to sit down and talk with students, to visit with faculty members, department by department. One faculty member put it to me neatly one day. He reached me by phone and, in a slow bass voice, intoned, "Like God, I know you are there, but I never see you in our part of the world." He didn't mean to hurt. He was just expressing the truth. There was so little time.
Former independent college president

The age when major public university presidents leave office does not reflect a pattern different from that of other public college executives. Seven percent remained in office past age sixty-five and 13 percent left office when they reached sixty-five years of age. The midcareer change phenomenon was also at work with this group, as shown by the 57 percent who moved to some other activity between the ages of fifty and sixty-four. Finally, 64 percent of the NASULGC presidents changed positions between the ages of thirty-five and forty-nine years.

Independent Colleges and Universities

Not unlike their counterparts in the public sector, presidents of most independent colleges and universities moved out of that office and into a variety of interesting postpresidential activities. The former presidents of nearly 1,400 private institutions were included in this study, and 774 of them returned usable responses.

As most higher education observers know, NAICU represents a heterogeneous array of institutions that range from small, church-related liberal arts colleges to sprawling, multipurpose research universities. To reflect some of these differences, NAICU institutions were grouped according to enrollment, and the commentary that follows differentiates between small, midsize, and large institutions. The first group includes from 428 NAICU colleges that enrolled fewer than 1,000 students. The second category includes a total of 322 institutions of from 1,000-10,000 students. The third group includes twenty-four universities that enrolled over 10,000 students.

As in the public sector, some independent college presidents end their presidential careers under difficult circumstances. Among responses from institutions in this group was one that read, "The position held now by our former president is unknown." Another college reported, "We don't know his whereabouts nor what he is doing." Three other colleges merely said that the address of their former president was unknown, and four others indicated that their former presidents were undecided about their futures at the time of the survey.

Worse yet were reports about two former presidents, each of whom had served in office less than two years. The first was "under indictment awaiting trial for a number of charges associated with misuse of funds of this institution." The second "tried to establish a nontraditional college," according to the respondent, who continued, "The last I heard, he was cleaning carpets, and once it was reported he was organizing unemployed academics to do household services." So much for horror stories.

In earlier times, former presidents of independent colleges and universities may have returned to the classroom, but that does not appear to be the case now. Only 16 percent of all former NAICU presidents included in the study returned to teaching. This move occurred more often in the largest institutions, where one-third of the presidents reverted to professorial status.

Fewer independent college presidents moved from one presidency to another than did their counterparts in the public sector. Only 11 percent of the NAICU presidents did so, but, again, this happened among presidents of large institutions more often than it did among presidents of small or midsized colleges. The same pattern was evident in the case of former presidents who took other kinds of administrative positions in academe. Only 13 percent of the total group of NAICU presidents became vice presidents, deans, alumni directors, development officers, board chairpersons, assistants to the president, or similar campus officers.

Full retirement was the choice of 14 percent of the entire group. Few major university presidents picked this option although more than twice as many presidents of midsized institutions did so. Perhaps more interesting postcareer opportunities are available to the presidents of larger, better-known institutions, a contention supported by the data on presidents who entered semiretirement. In all, 7 percent of the group were semiretired, but nearly twice as many major university presidents were in this category. Clearly, they chose to combine a limited retirement with some other form of professional or personal activity, including consulting, writing (in some cases, writing a history of the college), preaching, fund raising, lecturing, or teaching. In several instances, the semiretired president was named chancellor of the institution and assumed some concomitant duties.

By far the most popular choice of employment among former NAICU presidents was a position outside academe. Thirty-one percent made this choice, but it was an option more popular among presidents of small colleges than of large institutions. No doubt this was because many small colleges are church-related and tend to select presidents from among the clergy. When presidential duties end, the obvious move for these persons is back to some form of religious work. In fact, 83 of 150 small-college presidents did so, as did presidents of 39 out of 89 midsized institutions. None of the 24 major university presidents, however, chose this postpresidential route.

Other former NAICU presidents found interesting things to do, from farming to foreign affairs. One was appointed Secretary of Defense, several became presidents or staff members of foundations, many entered business or industry, others practiced law, became consultants, administered lower schools, headed associations or consortia, or worked for state and federal government agencies. Seven former presidents of private institutions became executive officers of state associations of independent colleges and universities, and three were named to state higher education positions. Others directed museums, concertized, sculpted, lectured. One became a farmer.

Despite reports that many independent colleges are closing, some private institutions are relatively young, and six of these, all with less than 1,000 students, said their founding presidents were still in office. The mortality rates for independent college presidents still in office were uniform across the three subgroups, averaging 5 percent. However, a much higher proportion of major university presidents died between the time they left office and the time of the survey—12 percent as compared with 5 percent for midsized colleges and only 4 percent for small colleges.

The highest earned degree of most independent college and university presidents in this sample was a doctorate, the Ph.D. for 51 percent. When all other doctoral degrees (Ed.D., Th.D., D.D., J.D., LL.D., and M.D.) were added to that figure, the total was over 60 percent. Another 21 percent held master's degrees, and 8 percent reportedly had earned only bachelor's degrees. Again, smaller colleges differed from larger universities in that more presidents of colleges under 1,000 students had advanced degrees in religion or theology, and more smaller institutions selected presidents without doctorates or any graduate degrees at all.

The factor that appears to differentiate most clearly independent college presidents from those in the public sector was the major field of academic training. Nearly three out of every ten studied philosophy, theology, or religion, again reflecting the heavy concentration of clergy in small college presidencies. Twenty percent of all the presidents majored in the humanities, but in this field the larger institutions were more heavily represented. Education was the field of study for 17 percent of the total group, social science and physical sciences/mathematics each claimed 12 percent, 4 percent came from business, 3 percent from law, and 2 percent from the biological sciences. All other fields accounted for 9 percent of the former presidents.

A look at the prior position of these former NAICU presidents reveals an inverse relationship between size of institution and tendency to select presidents from outside. Twenty-nine percent of these former NAICU presidents moved from some nonacademic position into the president's office. But more than a third of the colleges under

1,000 students selected presidents from outside academe. Only 22 percent of midsized institutions and 8 percent of large universities selected presidents who were not then on campus.

An obvious explanation for this influx of nonacademics to independent college presidencies is that many smaller campuses are church related. The data show that one-fifth of small college presidents came directly from religious positions, as did almost one-tenth of the presidents who headed midsized institutions. With the exception of school administrators who were often heads of parochial school systems, no other pattern emerged from an examination of prepresidential backgrounds. Some came from business (a corporate executive), government (assistant secretary of the Navy), the arts (a concert pianist), and the nonprofit sector (a foundation officer). Still others were military officers, museum directors, judges, consultants, YMCA directors, researchers, artists, and librarians.

The deanship was the most promising internal stepping stone for aspiring independent college presidents. In all, 20 percent moved directly from the dean's office to the president's. Surprisingly, the next most promising spot was that of professor: 17 percent of the total sample gave up the blackboard for the executive suite. Only 11 percent of these had been vice presidents immediately prior to their presidencies, and only 10 percent had held other presidencies. Five percent were department heads, and 6 percent had held other academic positions.

Longevity in office appeared common among many independent college presidents. A substantial number served as president for twenty years or more. Two served their institutions for forty years each, and another for thirty-nine. At the other extreme, there appeared to be a rapid turnover of presidents early in their executive careers. Fifteen served for only one year, forty-nine served for two years, sixty-two for three years, and fifty-one left office after four years. Some of these short terms were served by interim or acting presidents.

In general, however, independent college presidents served substantial terms. Thirty-nine percent served for five to ten years, 26 percent held office from eleven to twenty years, and 11 percent served more than twenty years as institutional heads. These proportions were relatively constant for small, midsized, and large institutions.

Finally, data were collected on the ages at which these former independent college presidents left office. Many (17 percent) stayed in office beyond the conventional retirement age—more than twice the proportion of public college presidents who did so. Presidents of small and midsized colleges displayed amazing longevity. The senior member of this group left office at age eighty-two, two others did so at eighty-one, another at eighty, a baker's dozen remained in office during their seventies, and twenty-one of them chose age seventy as the time to hang up the academic robes.

The remaining independent college presidents tended to leave office about the same time as did their public sector colleagues. Eight percent retired at age sixty-five, 47 percent made midcareer moves between ages fifty and sixty-five, 19 percent found other jobs between ages forty and forty-nine, and only 2 percent left a presidency prior to reaching the age of forty years.

PART II
AFTER THE PRESIDENCY

One of the saving graces for new presidents is that they can't possibly know ahead of time how well they will do in some cases and how magnificently they will bomb in others.
Former liberal arts college president

Early chapters of this book portrayed a generation of college and university presidents both collectively and classified by the kinds of institutions they administered. Many facts emerged about former presidents and about what they did when their presidential duties ended. Although the statistics are interesting, numbers alone cannot tell the whole story of what lies beyond the presidency. Therefore, Part II draws from anecdotes to provide a more personalized account of what former presidents do and how they like doing it.

Some presidents missed the feeling of chalk dust on their hands and longed to experience again the excitement and drudgery of being a professor. This group returned to the highs and lows of teaching—to stimulating exchanges in seminar rooms, theses and term papers that "never would have gotten by when I was in college," and long department faculty meetings in which every possible nit was picked. Thus, chapter three chronicles thoughts of former presidents who are now "just another member of the faculty."

Many of these presidents, however, seem to have had administration in their blood. Apparently, they thrive on the alternating pleasure and hassle of administrative responsibilities. Hence, Chapter 4 discusses presidents who moved to other leadership positions in higher education. Of course, their real reasons for jumping back into the fray are difficult to uncover. Some presidents may have just wanted to climb another mountain; others may have feared trying to catch up in their academic fields, while still others probably preferred administrative visibility to the cloister of a faculty office. Some of these presidents may have been too young to retire, too ambitious to rest on past achievements, too eager to atone for earlier disasters, or too administratively talented to be laid on the shelf. Their comments provide some insight into how midcareer change affects academic executives.

Politicians and business persons often remind academics about the "real world" out there. The jibe wrongly implies, of course, that the walls of ivy separate doers (in the "real world") from thinkers (in academe). This study has already demonstrated, however, that the real world is full of former college and university administrators who are doing important and interesting things. Chapter 5 discusses these presidents who found new career opportunities outside the academic world.

Concluding Part II is a chapter devoted to former college and university presidents who elected either limited or full retirement. Again, anecdotes from respondents in these categories help to illuminate life after the presidency. Naturally, most respondents who contributed these insights were older, certainly more seasoned, presumably wiser. Their comments enrich our understanding of the presidency, what it demands of those who serve in it, and what treasures it hides.

What happens after the presidency? The question can be resoundingly answered: a great deal!

PART II: AFTER THE PRESIDENCY

THREE

Just Another Member of the Faculty
Returning to the Classroom

There were some aspects of the presidency I enjoyed. I had a wonderful, old-fashioned office which I really liked. I enjoyed being the Big Wheel, at least for a time. Until the novelty wore off, I enjoyed having "made it," being asked to speak to groups, associating with other wheels. But all of that paled after about four years for whatever reason. . . . It was mostly a matter of getting tired of it, and the fact that I spent three-quarters of my time doing what I didn't like and one-quarter doing what I did like. Now the situation is reversed. But I still miss that lovely old office.
State college president who returned to teaching

One tired academic joke asserts, "Old presidents never die: they just lose their faculties." The truth is, however, that few faculties regain their old presidents. As the data reported in earlier chapters demonstrate, for every former president who returns to teaching, there are six or seven others who head in other directions.

Comments from former presidents who resumed classroom chores provide many insights into the academic enterprise, the office of president, and teaching itself. Following are excerpts from responses (many of them handwritten) to a series of survey questions.[1]

Why Return to Teaching?

Among all the reasons former presidents give for returning to teaching, the most frequently voiced is also the most emotional. They speak of teaching in almost amorous terms, as if it were a long-lost sweetheart. It is a matter of love, often first love, and the language they use clearly reflects this affection. One former president wrote:

What a wonderful way to spend one's years! Teaching was my first love and it will always be. Teaching is, in fact, a kind of loving, a way of sharing. I find it pure joy.

Other presidents surveyed based their decision to resume teaching on a somewhat broader, yet still emotional, attachment to the institution and to the academic community in general. A desire to "continue giving something back" to the college motivated one former president to take a faculty position. Another said he returned to teaching because

I am deeply committed to the academic enterprise and was eager to have more time for teaching and to complete research and writing that I had begun but had to put aside when I was president.

Some administrators conceptualized their administrative activities in terms of teaching. The former chancellor of a public university campus put it this way:

I returned to teaching because I always conceived of myself as a teacher. As chancellor I learned a bit more about some new dimensions of teaching.

A substantial number of former presidents tended to idealize professorial status and freedom. For them, being a professor meant much more than just being a teacher. One said it in no uncertain terms: "There is no better role in any college or university than that of full professor."

1. Here I acknowledge the assistance of Norma Melcolm and Leslie A. Francis, Jr., graduate students in higher education administration at the University of Maryland at College Park, who conducted the follow-up study of former presidents who returned to teaching.

Many others considered working closely with students as the basic justification for directing their attention toward the classroom. A frequent response was, "It is satisfying to help students grow intellectually, and perhaps personally, too." This concern for student development and growth also turned up as an important but somewhat ancillary reason given by several former presidents who placed other considerations first. One of these was scholarship. For some, the difficulty of producing any substantial scholarly contributions while serving in the presidency clearly was a dominant factor. For example, one respondent admitted

[I] had four or five books in mind that I wanted to write before retirement, and I knew that the only way I could complete those books would be to get back into teaching. I had no interest in government or industry. Certainly, I did not want any other administrative job in higher education.

This lack of interest in business or government employment was another theme. Only the president quoted above, however, openly expressed his distaste for accepting a job in those two realms. Frequently, former presidents expressed a sense that perhaps they had not been well placed in the head office and had really been diverted from earlier, more pleasurable pursuits. These feelings were expressed by a man who had administered a small liberal arts college as well as a major university:

I returned to teaching, which had always been my first love, after twenty-two years of academic administration. I did so partly because I like the role of teacher-scholar and partly because I felt I was not well suited to the administrative role as times changed.

Finally, some former presidents elected to return to the classroom because they were unhappy with administrative pressures and teaching offered a haven. After serving four years as president of a small college, one respondent wrote:

I was nearing the end of my professional career (chronologically), and I thought it made sense for me to return to the classroom and round things out there. Four years in the presidency was enough for one who had not trained for, planned, or contemplated such a job. I did enjoy many aspects of the responsibility. I enjoyed least the stupid griping of arrogant faculty members and the senseless requirements (demands) of HEW. I also tired of the problems associated with students having no business in college.

As such comments suggest, both negative and positive feelings motivate former college and university presidents to resume their professional careers. Some return to the classroom seeking a lost love; others hope to avoid the bureaucratic headaches of the presidency. However, relatively few presidents actually elected this route, and the next section discusses some of the reasons.

Problems for Returning Teachers

Becoming a professor again may not be all sweetness and light. Some former presidents who moved back into faculty ranks clearly experienced a reentry shock. For example, former presidents often rediscover with a jolt that, as faculty members, they must devote a good deal of their time to doing their own clerical work. "No longer having a secretary or even a personal office telephone" bothered one returnee, and the absence of someone to type letters and file papers was mentioned by many others.

A less concrete but probably more frustrating problem was articulated by an obviously thoughtful former president who identified a major difficulty of being able to "focus on issues that are narrow enough to constitute research of the sort that a professor can do."

Another former president addressed the same issue in a somewhat different manner. He wrote:

It is difficult to view the narrow problems of a traditional course as challenging and stimulating after wrestling daily with complex situations, the resolutions of which have widespread impact.

A slightly different slant was provided by another president-cum-teacher. This respondent moved the discussion along to a problem frequently mentioned in the responses—catching up in the academic field. Here is how he described the difficulty:

The reentry into teaching is difficult. There is both a mental and physical readjustment. The mental is easier than the physical. By physical, I mean lack of travel, lack of the telephone ringing constantly, lack of a constant stream of visitors, and lack of minute-by-minute pressure. There is, of course, the usual difficulty of getting back up to speed in your academic field and gaining acceptance again as a competent person in the discipline.

An even stronger and more negative view of the problem of catching up was voiced this way:

It is impossible to go back. Students change, knowledge advances, and colleagues are different. It is not a reentry, it is an entry. Failure to anticipate this causes disappointment.

Fortunately, some former presidents anticipated the problem or made arrangements to soften the blow. The president of one state university reported:

I continued to teach one undergraduate course throughout my fifteen years as president. I encountered no difficulties in reentry because I had been teaching all along and had kept up on part of my field. I did have a great deal of reading and catching up in recent scholarship to feel completely adequate in graduate instruction and directing master's and doctoral theses.

When his institution gave him a period of leave following appointment of a successor, one public university president used it to good advantage. He commented:

I am not aware of any significant difficulties encountered upon reentry into teaching after the presidency. I had considerable catching up to do in my academic field, but this was eased by a six-month sabbatical.

The reentry problem was best summed up by the respondent who admitted:

There was a general adjustment to gearing and slowing the pace. One had some time to plan a day instead of having it planned for you. Actually, the faculty received me better than I expected. The first year I had a tremendous amount of reading to do ... but it got done.

So much for problems. The positive side is the gratification many former presidents found in their new duties.

Satisfaction in the Classroom

Regardless of their reasons for resuming teaching and the problems involved, the former presidents who returned to teaching were almost unanimous in expressing their delight with being back in the heart of the academic world. As one put it:

Teaching is more satisfying than being president because you are working first hand at what education is all about. You can see changes in students.

Another tended to express his satisfaction in a somewhat left-handed manner. He wrote:

I certainly like the subject matter I deal with now as compared to the Mickey Mouse of schedules, budgets, rules, memos, building problems, educational trivia in general, having to be nice to people I often didn't like very much, etc. Perhaps it is that teaching is a positive thing while so much of administration is at least regulatory, even punitive sometimes.

One man summed it all up most cogently. He held not one but three presidencies in the course of a 28-year career in higher education. No doubt he speaks for the vast majority of academic executives who elected to finish out their careers as they had begun them—as teacher, adviser, and scholar. His insightful comments contrasting the presidency to the classroom provide an appropriate conclusion to this section:

I like the leadership role. It consumed me, and I did not "miss teaching," as so many administrators aver. I enjoyed the limelight and counting for something in policy making and seeing the enterprise grow and progress. Very satisfying. But I had all of that my ego required and now cherish the satisfaction of reading more deeply, being again part of the faculty in an intimate way, and teaching about American government and about the politics of higher education. Totally satisfying.

PART II: AFTER THE PRESIDENCY

FOUR

Back into the Fray
Taking Another Administrative Position in Higher Education

The fun has gone out of being an administrator at the top in higher education. The revenues are not sufficient. Faculty companionship has been replaced by divisiveness, union talk, down-with-the-establishment,"me only" initiatives.
Former liberal arts college president

An awareness is growing in America that midcareer change is perfectly normal, often desirable. In American higher education, the practice of making a substantial—in some cases, even dramatic—shift in career direction is common. As any president watcher can tell you, chief administrators of our colleges and universities play the career-change game as well as any other professionals.

The next chapter of this book will focus on presidents who decide that opportunity lies outside the academic community. In this chapter, however, will be examined the group of college and university presidents who continue their administrative careers within academe or, in some cases, at its fringes.[1]

Taking another administrative position in higher education is, by a slight margin, the most popular form of career change followed by

---

1. The efforts of another of my graduate students produced a portion of the material used here. Michael J. Worth, a doctoral student in higher education administration at the University of Maryland at College Park, conducted a follow-up study of presidents who assumed another presidency; his survey responses appear in this chapter.

39

presidents who leave office. Actually, of the more than 1,400 presidents surveyed, 26 percent chose this route. It should not surprise most readers that over two hundred of these presidents moved on to another presidency or became executive officers of college or university systems. What is surprising is that 161 others assumed lower administrative positions on campus or found jobs off campus in enterprises closely related to academe.

What motivates so many institutional leaders to pack up, pick up, and move on? Quite likely, the reasons are diverse and, in some cases, too painful to share, even in an unsigned questionnaire. For some presidents, however, the motivation was clearly the nexus of opportunity and ambition—the chance to move up by moving on. For others, particularly those who made a lateral move, the determining factors were probably environmental. They heard sweeter music elsewhere and succumbed to the lure. Unfortunately, some presidents moved on for less happy reasons—exhaustion, frustration, personal mischance.

In this chapter, as before, actual testimony from college and university presidents will illustrate the new career directions that some took and their reasons for doing so.

Positions on the Fringe

Many challenging professional activities capture the administrative interests of former college and university presidents. Although some of these activities are beyond the walls of ivy, they are too closely related to academic interests to be characterized as nonacademic. State governmental agencies concerned with higher education fall within this cluster, as do higher education associations, educational consortia, and local school systems. Many presidents covered in this survey found professional opportunities in such organizations.

Six former presidents became state commissioners of higher education (one had the title of chancellor), and three others took staff positions with statewide coordinating boards. Another assumed leadership of a statewide higher education planning commission. Interestingly, two of these commissioners had been presidents of private institutions prior to being appointed to public sector positions. Making the transition from campus to statewide leadership was both difficult and attractive. As one commissioner put it:

In a position like this, your perspective changes. It has to—otherwise you belong on a campus. The chance to help meet the educational needs of an entire state was an opportunity I couldn't turn down.

Grappling with education problems on behalf of members of an education association became an alternative career for eight former presidents. Serving as executive director (sometimes called president, too) or staff member of these Washington-based associations appeared to offer former presidents wider horizons while permitting them to stay in the field they knew best. As one former president who now directs an association said, "Ten years as a president was enough. After two years I began repeating myself."

Maintaining contact with his original professional field motivated the departure of one major public university president. He explained his move to a national health policy organization in this way:

The most important reason in my leaving the university presidency was professional. At the time of accepting the offer to become president, I informed the regents that I would be president for no less than five and no more than seven years, since I did not want to lose touch with my profession and basic interests.

A negative reason for exchanging the president's suite for an association office was given by the former state college president who wrote:

My presidential salary was "frozen" for three years, which harmed my retirement and didn't fully compensate my contributions as a successful college administrator. I became disgusted and discouraged while bureaucratic and governmental regulations and administrative intrusion added to the enervating requirements of the position.

Several other former presidents found interesting professional challenge as leaders of consortia or of statewide college associations. For the most part, these individuals had been presidents of independent colleges although one former community college president assumed leadership of a statewide association of community colleges. These presidents found meaningful professional outlets for their talents within the field of higher education, but they were able to put behind them the daily pressures of campus administration.

Finally, some former presidents assumed new responsibilities in education but not specifically in higher education. Usually, they accepted positions in public elementary or secondary school systems, often as superintendent of schools. Several, however, became principals, and three others were appointed as chief state school officers. One, a former community college president, gave the following reasons for turning away from higher education:

> *I became disillusioned with the community college philosophy not being either attained or worked towards. I saw an open-door philosophy in regard to admissions, but I did not see the extra effort, programs, or even concern for correcting deficiencies of students admitted with low academic standards.*

Another president who returned to administration in the public schools also reported disillusionment with the academic scene but placed the blame on his state's political climate. He wrote:

> *I ran into a philosophy almost directly opposed to my own when an ultraliberal governor was elected. Since I was president of a state-owned college, the factions were strongly felt. The governor handled himself with a team of people so liberal that some were clearly radical and others bordered on that category. Personnel practices became so loose that erratic and even illegal faculty behavior was tolerated and could not be controlled.*

Such negative motivations are probably atypical of why some college presidents moved on to other education tasks. Usually, they relinquished office because opportunity beckoned. One university system executive, for example, was appointed U.S. Commissioner of Education and later headed an education foundation. In another instance, a community college president was picked to head the community college unit of his state's department of education. Whatever the reason, these former presidents made midcareer changes that permitted them to continue serving in education. Many of them, it appears, placed the office of president in a broad education perspective and, in so doing, moved on to (or back to) education endeavors they found more satisfying and more worthy of their talents.

Other Campus Positions

Just over 5 percent of this generation of former presidents moved from the president's office to some subordinate position on campus or on another campus. For some of these people the move provided a graceful and useful way to culminate an administrative career. As one member of this group confided:

I had been fighting the big battles long enough, but I wanted to continue contributing to this institution. Thus, I decided to step out of the line of fire and to work on fund raising until it was time to retire.

Almost all these presidential veterans stayed at the institution they once headed and engaged in an interesting array of activities. In the major public universities, for example, three former presidents took over direction of international programs, another became director of development, and one assumed leadership of a cancer research unit. Growing interest in fund raising at state colleges is exemplified by three former AASCU presidents who turned their attention to that activity. Four other presidents of public colleges directed academic or research units, two became assistants to presidents, and one headed his institution's international program. One former AASCU president became director of a conference center, and another took over the Washington office of a state college system.

Community college presidents who moved to other administrative positions selected equally diverse roles. Three served as assistants to community college campus or system heads, and one became an assistant vice president of a university system. Other positions assumed by these former community college presidents included comptroller, business manager, dean of continuing education, director of a "productivity center," associate dean, and academic counselor.

Former presidents from the private sector, as might be expected, had even more opportunity to explore fund raising. Nine campus development offices were taken over by former presidents, another president became the grants coordinator on his campus, and two others administered alumni programs. Three former private college presidents chose to continue in administration as presidential assistants. Three others became continuing education directors, two directed institutional research, and two more became library directors.

Two devoted their time to coordinating campus religious activities. Titles of positions assumed by other former private college presidents included director of international programs, admissions director, public relations officer, associate provost, director of graduate studies, and director of special events.

An academic or student affairs deanship beckoned twenty-seven former college and university presidents. Some had been student affairs deans before becoming presidents. For others, the position was a new role because they had moved directly to the presidency without intervening experience as a dean. The move from president to dean was made by presidents of private colleges, community colleges, and four-year state colleges, but not by any major public university president in the sample.

On the other hand, presidents from all types of institutions did step down into vice presidential offices. Thirty-nine individuals identified in the study assumed vice presidential duties including academic affairs, planning, development, general administration, finance, and student affairs. The motivation behind moving from the number one spot to a cabinet position in another president's administration undoubtedly varies from individual to individual. One former president explained his move in this manner:

After a while the fatigue factor sets in, but that wasn't the major reason. For one thing, I was tired of fighting with my board over the direction of the institution. I decided on taking my current position because here you don't have to take all the flack you do in a presidency. You don't pick up the evening paper to find out what kind of an SOB you have been today.

Another simply said:

The idea of being a president is more satisfying than is being one. I really feel more creative in my new role, and more satisfied, too.

Some former presidents found interesting and useful things to do in campus positions below the level of president. Others moved to positions that are less understood by traditional academicians. In the public sector these positions are in systemwide or statewide administrative units; in the private sector these positions are often honorary or related to campus governance.

Getting Promoted

Presidents of private colleges and universities have a postpresidential option that does not appear open to public institutional heads—moving up to chairman of the board. In three small private colleges and one large university, the former president became board chairman. The institutions surveyed gave no further information about the duties of their board members, but it can be assumed that the duties were both ceremonial and administrative (policy making). (It would be interesting to discover how these former presidents made the transition from administration to governance. An equally fascinating question is how the current presidents of these institutions felt about operating under the watchful eyes of their predecessors.)

Yet another practice unique to the private sector is that of elevating the president to chancellor. The promotion appears common, especially in smaller institutions. Generally, the former president assumes full-time responsibility for fund raising and development activities, leaving internal academic matters to a successor. The logic of such a move appears sound: former presidents are well established in the community and with the alumni and thus should know about untapped resources. (Unfortunately, little is known about how well this works in practice.)

In the public sector, campus executives often move to positions in system administrations. Although generally considered a promotion, such a move is often denigrated by some academicians who see these superordinate administrative levels as necessary evils at best. The reasons for assuming a system leadership position are clear, however, and are best explained by one president who listed, as his primary reason for moving up, the opportunity to contribute more to higher education in his state. He reported:

When it became obvious that there was going to be a change in our administrative structure, I had to decide whether I would be happy working for someone else or happier as the chancellor. Had the governance change not occurred or had the board not chosen me, I'm sure I would have remained as president and quite happy in my duties.

This practice of leaving a presidency to become system head occurs in community college systems as well as in systems that include state colleges and major research universities. Sometimes private institutional presidents are even afforded this opportunity. The former president of a small southern college became vice chancellor of a large state system and, in another instance, the president of a private university took over a midwestern, multicampus, public university system. Commenting on this move, he said:

These two jobs—system head and campus head—are quite different. In addition, the public university has many more active constituent groups to which the president must respond, and the public university's business is conducted in the open arena much more than is the business of the private university. There is, however, no major reason inhibiting the transfer of an administrator and of administrative skills from one sector to the other.

The notion that administrative talent can be transferred from one institution to another is apparently widely accepted in higher education. Many presidents leave one presidency to assume another. Comments from presidents who made this kind of midcareer change are reported in the following section.

From One Presidency to Another

Greater opportunity looms large as a primary factor in the decision of a college or university president to move on to a second, even third, presidency. One president moved to another institution because it offered more "challenge and a stronger foundation for development as an academic institution." Yet another was motivated by his religious faith and a long-standing dream of the "opportunity to build a new Christian graduate university." For a third, both personal and professional factors were important:

The strongest factor which influenced my decision to make the change was probably emotional since I am an alumnus of the college I now serve. Also, my father was president of this college twenty-five years ago. The other factors which impacted my decision were increased size and scope of the work.

Geography also appears to be an important consideration in presidential decisions to move. One president said he preferred being close to a major eastern metropolitan center, and another satisfied his geographical preferences by moving in the opposite direction. His current campus, he admitted, was

in a much more pleasant setting; a college in the midwest is perceptibly different in its attitude and value system than a college in greater [a major eastern city].

Even adversity was a positive factor to some. A president who assumed a second presidency relished the challenge and greater visibility in his new position, as well as the greater freedom ("local autonomy," he called it) at the new campus:

Fewer students, more graduate students, larger branch system, larger budget, larger library, more local autonomy, and far, far more problems. The president has greater responsibility because he has to work directly with a board. This place also has a faculty union, a poor sports program, and heavy competition from nearby urban universities. The president is much more in the limelight and has greater social requirements.

Some presidents move on to another presidency because they perceive their work at the first institution is done. A private university president who was in his second presidency remarked:

I felt that I had moved [university X] as far as I could in the near term. In so doing, I made some unpopular decisions but, even in retrospect, proper decisions which occasioned internal trauma. I did, however, leave [it] in good shape.

He listed other factors that encouraged him to take the new presidency:

the aggressive recruitment of the search committee and the firm belief that what was happening here was terribly important and that I was pretty well equipped philosophically to head such an institution.

In most cases, the trouble experienced by presidents seems to arise from governing boards rather than faculty. When asked to explain why they moved to another institution, several presidents mentioned problems with trustees. One, whose board presented him with "an invitation to resign," sought a "more cohesive, supportive board," and another found both the campus atmosphere and the board chairman hard to take. He reported:

> *[The institution I left] had no church affiliation, and virtually any kind of behavior was tacitly permitted. [I am an abstemious Quaker, and] some of the officials at the previous school thought I was out of place there. Perhaps I was.*

According to this president, the chairman of the board was a

> *hard-drinking, hard-smoking, tough-talking, super-aggressive woman who probably thought I was a man from Mars. We finally quit communicating, especially when I learned that she was holding rump sessions of the board off campus without my knowledge.*

An even more drastic indictment of a board came from the former president of a college that had elected trustees. Citing what he called "incompetence and malmotivation" of the board, he explained:

> *No qualifications exist to stand for election and, thus, completely inexperienced and unprepared trustees often attain membership. Having no understanding about education or management, and having personal aggrandizements and/or fancied political ambitions as their motivations, their activities are decidedly more harmful than helpful. As I viewed the board of trustees at the new institution, it appeared that these shortcomings were far less severe.*

But escaping to a new institution does not always mean that the situation improves. One president was troubled by the problems of dealing with a unionized faculty. He recalled:

> *As president of my previous institution, I spent the majority of my time managing the institution in accordance with collegial procedures. At my present institution ... I find myself spending literally hours each week dealing with interpretations of contract language in the administration of the collective bargaining agreements. My ability to provide educational leadership for the institution is, I believe, impaired by the amount of time and effort that must be devoted to contract administration.*

As these remarks testify, life for college or university presidents is hard. Yet, in spite of problems, a great many presidents continue in that vocation, and a great many more stay close to presidential offices even when they no longer carry that title. It seems they are able to rise above negative factors: excitement overcomes fatigue, satisfaction rises above frustration, success exceeds failure, recognition and respect surpass contempt and criticism. When the positive factors outweigh the negatives, then the presidents move "back into the fray" of administration, often in a new place and with a new title and, generally, with renewed enthusiasm for the tasks at hand.

Challenges of another kind face those former presidents who turn away from the academic world to take positions in government, the world of business, or the nonprofit sector. The next chapter documents these midcareer changes.

PART II: AFTER THE PRESIDENCY

FIVE

Into the Real World
Moving to Industry, Government, or the Nonprofit Sector

Being a college president is like spading a flower bed for your wife when you would rather be sailing. It's an honor, and you are glad she is happy, but, damn, you'd rather be out on the lake.
Former liberal arts college president

Some critics of higher education fault the academic environment for its detachment from the mainstream of American society. References to the so-called ivory tower are always depreciative, and academics are often summarily dismissed by moguls of industry or government. Of course, in many cases there is good reason for such treatment. Higher education has more than its share of bright, able people who have "never met a payroll," as some business executives are fond of pointing out. In all fairness, however, these critics insist on ignoring the fact that most academicians based their careers on priorities other than payrolls and profits. Even so, evidence suggests that many academics, particularly those who once served as presidents of colleges and universities, do well in the real world.

This chapter discusses what these former presidents did after leaving academe, why they decided to venture into a new world, how their presidencies compared with other jobs, and how they felt about the possibility of returning to academe.[1]

1. Thanks are due Jon H. Larson and Edward T. Brenner, graduate students in higher education administration at the University of Maryland at College Park, for material they contributed to this chapter.

Nonacademic Opportunities

Just under 25 percent of the 1,406 former college and university presidents surveyed not only left office, but left campus as well. For reasons that will be revealed later, they found new, apparently more interesting, and usually more lucrative employment in other sectors of the economy. They provided evidence that the academic experience, particularly in administration, hones skills that can be useful in nonacademic enterprises.

Severing campus ties was more prevalent among former presidents of private than of public colleges. While only about one-fourth of the latter took nonacademic jobs, the proportion of private college presidents who did so was nearly one out of three. It should be recalled, however, that many private college presidents were members of the clergy and, when they left office, most took up other religious duties. Many returned to the pulpit, and others assumed titles ranging from prioress to pastor, archivist to archbishop, business manager to bishop. Former private college presidents who were not members of the clergy found employment in a wide variety of secular settings. Many became associated with banks and financial institutions. Others, including one who became Secretary of Defense, turned to state or federal government service. Business, law, consulting, association work, and the arts attracted other private college presidents who made midcareer moves out of academe.

The future was equally promising for public sector presidents who opted for new careers away from campus. For example, former NASULGC presidents found positions in business (president of Dun and Bradstreet, chairman of the board at General Computing), in government (secretary of human resources in Kansas, administrator of NASA, executive officer of Radio Free Europe, ambassador to Sweden), as well as in the nonprofit sector (president of Resources for the Future, president of the Corporation for Public Broadcasting, executive officer of the Center for Study of Democratic Institutions, and chairman of the board of the Los Angeles Times Mirror Company). In all, 25 percent of those who had once headed major public universities selected nonacademic positions.

State college presidents seemed, by a good margin, to favor positions in government. They served in federal agencies (HEW, EPA, and the Department of Transportation) and in state offices (the Kentucky senate, lieutenant governorship of Michigan, the cabinet secretariat for administration in Wisconsin, a similar office in Pennsylvania, Civil Service Commission in Michigan, and the governor's staff in North Carolina).[2] Also included in the 14 percent of former AASCU presidents who left the academic world were those who managed smaller corporate enterprises, served as vice presidents in larger corporations, or managed their own consulting firms.

Consulting was a popular postpresidential activity for former community college presidents. One was self-employed, and others entered business careers (involving recreation vehicles, real estate, life insurance, trucking, carpet manufacturing, and a savings and loan association). Relatively few in this group found government positions although one was elected to the Oregon state legislature. Also included in the 13 percent of former community college presidents who took nonacademic positions was a person who headed a community foundation in New York, another who became president of a Michigan osteopathic hospital, and a third who directed a museum of history and industry in Seattle.

Clearly, college and university presidents are a good source of executive talent. This recognition of executive ability among academic executives may not dispel the ivory tower myth, but it does support the contention that their administrative responsibilities do not differ markedly from those of executives in nonacademic organizations.

Why Leave Academe?

Presidents who left office to try their luck in the nonacademic world were amazingly candid in reporting why they decided to leave. Their reasons were personal as well as professional, ranging from boredom to a sense that their major work had been completed. "I had completed the major thrust of my professional goals for the college," said one former president. Adding a more personal note, he said:

My personal fulfillment requires a greater emphasis on reform of education and educational administration than satisfactions from daily management. I therefore became involved in research and applied research.

Similar feelings motivated another former president to respond as follows:

2. Another state college president, elected governor of Wisconsin, is not included above because the institution where he served as president did not respond to the survey.

I felt that in ten years I had rounded out my term—that is, I had achieved most of the objectives which were possible for me, and I discovered what ends were beyond my reach. I think there comes a time in any job when excitement and growth taper off, and to continue means you are just minding the store. It seemed to me the college could benefit from the leadership of a younger man to whom these matters could be a challenge rather than a burden.

Burdens convinced another college president that the time had come to try something new. He wrote:

I was dog tired. I was essentially successful, but to maintain that level of success would take increasingly more effort. Presidents get little help in relieving fatigue and maintaining academic timeliness.

In addition to the physical strain, a mental weariness overtakes some presidents. The former president of a small public university explained:

The most important reason for leaving the university environment was that I was starting to do things a second and third time, and it was getting boring. I needed some new challenges.

Genuine concern for the welfare of the institution—often combined with more personal reasons—motivates some presidents to pass on the duties of office to someone else. One president who found other things to do outside academe commented:

An institution deserves, indeed requires, new faces, new ideas, and new approaches. Seldom do institutions take the initiative in securing these needed changes. The capable leader is obligated to make it possible. Additionally, I wanted to force myself to try some new experiences to prove or disprove my ability to handle them.

Often personal reasons outweigh professional factors in a president's decision to leave. Prefacing his remarks with the observation that he had completed his original task of reorganizing a university, one respondent confided: "I had a large family in a small, upstate city, with extremely poor services for education, health, and protection."

The president of a small private college reached his decision to leave office following the untimely death of his wife. His departure from the academic world was perhaps the most daring and romantic of all:

I sold my house, furniture, and became a vagabond, sailing from Maine to Florida, the Virgin Islands, around the Brittany Coast, in the Mediterranean. After a year and a half I bought a sailboat to be my floating home. Shortly thereafter, I met, loved, married a marvelous woman who has adapted marvelously to the vagabond life.

The sea lured still another former president whose main reason for leaving office was reported earlier. He revealed:

On the personal side, my wife and I had long wanted to take off in our boat for some extended live-aboard cruising, and it seemed a good time to do this while I was still strong enough to haul a line. We took our boat down the intracostal waterway and cruised for three years in the Bahamas.

As the saying goes, "That's nice work if you can get it," but for most former college and university presidents, even those near the end of an active career, other professional chores beckoned. The president of one of this nation's most prestigious public university systems summed it up in these words:

I had served for seven and one-half difficult years, was sixty-five, within two years of mandatory retirement, and wanted to leave while it was possible to do something in my profession.

He associated himself with a public service organization that put his executive abilities to good use.

Not all presidents, however, leave because they have new and interesting things to do. Sometimes there is trouble, and the decision to leave is made in an effort to resolve a problem. That was exactly what happened in the case of a president who headed a small state university. He reported:

I became involved in a personal, classic power struggle with one member of the board. This involved such things as the desire of that regent to see certain second- and third-level employees dismissed. The rest of the board preferred not to become involved in what they considered to be a problem between the two of us, and so the struggle intensified. About two months before I resigned, I received a vote of confidence from the board. This served only to further intensify the struggle, and I resigned in an attempt to alleviate the vindictive actions which the dissident regent was preparing to take against several segments of the university. Only then did things settle down a little bit.

As a group, these presidents who bid farewell to their campuses and move on to other things are qualified to reflect on how a college presidency compares with other kinds of positions. Their reflections provide another glimpse of academic administrators.

Comparing the Presidency with Other Jobs

The question put to former college and university presidents who assumed nonacademic positions was simple: How would you rate your satisfaction with the job of president against other jobs you have had? Their responses were straightforward and diverse.

One former president summed it up in one word: "equal." Another, who now serves in a governor's cabinet, offered this perspective:

The job satisfaction of being president of a university is tremendous. It was greater than any job I had previously and about equal to the job I presently hold.

Being president was by "far the most satisfying" of his several jobs, according to one respondent whose words were typical of a great many other responses to the question. One respondent wholeheartedly agreed, but his thoughts turned to the satisfaction of another person close to the president. He wrote:

The job of a college president, of course, can and does have considerable satisfaction for the incumbent. I am not sure that this is equally true of the spouses, for of necessity the job demands their time and effort at tasks which generally would not have been of their own choosing.

In general, however, most of the cohort spoke glowingly of their presidential years. "The highlight of my experience," wrote one. He was joined by another who wrote, "Frankly, I had a ball," and by yet another who concluded:

I consider myself a very lucky fellow. I have enjoyed and felt rewarded in every position I have held, but my ten years as a president topped them all.

Often, the sense of involvement in something important translated into presidential satisfaction. This notion was best expressed by a public college president in the following:

The job of president brought more satisfaction than any job before or since. Even with all the pain, fatigue, disillusionment, etc., there is no substitute for the satisfaction which comes from knowing that you have been in a position to make a difference.

Some, however, recalled the presidency in less favorable terms. One former university president considered the job "interesting and challenging, but not as much fun" as his other positions. Two others found their earlier deanships more satisfying, and a third reported "greater satisfaction and influence in making meaningful changes" in his postpresidential position. This theme was eloquently stated by a president whose career had included teaching, administration, and government service. He wrote:

There is more satisfaction in a professional field, or in administering an organization where new ideas and new programs (instead of rehashing old ones) are more evident. Both of my jobs in government were more interesting. I guess I would even say that about the professional work I did as a professor.

Regardless of their assessment of presidential years, most former presidents would probably agree with their colleague who moved to a corporate vice presidency:

[I find it impossible to] rate my satisfaction with the presidency against what I am doing now. I would say, however, that I could not have gotten here without my prior experience, and I am glad to be here because it is a different set of responsibilities and challenges.

Returning to the Presidency

Another question elicited additional information about the college and university presidency. Would you, the survey asked, once again become a college president? Most who responded were not enthusiastic about that possibility.

Some former presidents were surprisingly blunt about the suggestion. "No," one declared, adding:

> *The drift to sameness and mediocrity in higher education does not provide excitement and challenge. The frontiers and growing edges in modern society reside in organizations and institutions where restraints, regulations, and retrenchment are minimal.*

Equally opposed to the thought of returning to the presidency was the respondent who explained:

> *An inordinate amount of my time had to be spent in overcoming the negative aspects of institutional politics (especially at the state level). As a researcher and consultant, [I associate] with leaders who desire meaningful change and are willing to invest time as well as money in the process.*

Three other former presidents expressed their feelings on the matter in more concise phrases. Their comments were:

> *The only thing I miss from my former office is my secretary.*
>
> *I have done all the different kinds of jobs in a university and prefer other things now.*
>
> *I would not consider going back. The reason is simple—I have already done it.*

A few former presidents saw merit in the idea of resuming presidential duties. In almost every case, however, there were conditions attached to the notion. One said:

> *I would consider returning, but at a level with less stress and fewer time demands. I thoroughly like the academic environment. It needs freeing from regulations, politics of faculty and government, and [it needs] a chance to be creative again.*

The respondents said they might consider returning, but only as professors. Another suggested an additional option:

> *I would like to return to the college environment but would prefer to do it either as the head of a university system or as a professor.*

Only one former president appeared to have actively sought another presidency. He reported:

I have had two offers. One was in a part of the country that does not appeal to me, and I turned it down primarily for that reason. The other was a one-year assignment which was very attractive but which, at the time, I could not accept.

Finally, the comments of two other former presidents revealed other compelling reasons why expatriates from presidential suites, especially those who have moved to the private sector, were not eager to resume presidential duties. Fewer constraints in nonacademic jobs was a recurring idea in the comments. One admitted:

Yes, I have considered another presidency, but maybe later. There are other things I want to do with the relative freedom I have as an engineer and management consultant.

Another respondent viewed a return to the presidency in economic terms. He wrote:

At some point in time I may return to the university environment. However, at this point in time my plans are indefinite; in any case, I would find it very expensive.

Evidence suggests, then, that former college and university presidents do quite well for themselves after they depart academe. They thrive and seem to like it. Or, perhaps more accurately, they find the nonacademic world compares favorably with what they experienced on campus. Of course, many of the presidents in the survey expressed mixed feelings: they valued their academic experiences but could not ignore the problems that crossed their desks. After their terms ended and they entered new worlds, the thought of returning to academe was not always easy to entertain.

PART II: AFTER THE PRESIDENCY

SIX

Getting the Gold Watch
Retirement and Semiretirement

In spite of all the joys in being a president, I much prefer what I am doing now—nothing. And I am still young. Will be seventy in June.
A retired state college president

According to retired and semiretired college and university presidents, hanging up the academic gown for good does not always afford former presidents a life of leisure. Contrary to the quote that opens this chapter, retirement appears to be a time of involvement in and continued contribution to their institutions and communities.

The pages that follow provide some insight into what former presidents actually do after retirement, how they plan for it, where they live, what new life styles they choose, and what events highlighted their presidential careers.[1]

It should be recalled that retirement or semiretirement was chosen by a relatively small proportion of presidents. Seven percent combined limited retirement with other activities, and 17 percent reported full retirement. Why? "An active presidency does not prepare one for retirement," wrote one former state university president. After a career of constant involvement, this generation of college and university presidents would not (perhaps, could not) idle away their greying years.

1. Materials for this chapter were provided by Jacqueline E. Johnson and Thomasine D. Guberski, graduate students in higher education administration at the University of Maryland at College Park.

Planning for Retirement

Although they filled their lives with activity, few retired presidents appear to have prepared very well for retirement. Several blamed their "narrow range of interests"—understandable, considering the demands of their positions—but this proved a hindrance when they at last had time for other things. The need to prepare for retirement was a recurring theme in the comments. One former president active in the National Retired Teachers Association said:

> *I began planning my retirement about five years before I retired. My plan was to work until sixty-five, but after much hassle with the state legislature, I felt maybe it was time for some fun.*

He offered this advice:

> *Begin to plan for the future. Join organizations with pre-retirement activities when you are about fifty-five, and develop a wide range of interests before you retire.*

Consequences of this failure to think carefully about what lies ahead were most dramatically revealed by a man who, during his long career, had administered three small colleges. He wrote:

> *I dislike retirement very much. I have always been a workaholic with few interests outside of the colleges where I have been president. Now I do much reading, some traveling and visiting friends. I like to have friends visit my home. I write many letters to relatives and friends. I frequently become depressed because I miss the young people, faculty, and staff. My feelings are of uselessness due to the fact that I have always been a builder.*

This former president called himself "a builder." Yet his remarks suggest that he was not a planner—at least not a planner of his own future.

Where Presidents Retire

An interesting phenomenon was revealed when current addresses of retired college and university presidents were examined: most of them stayed in or near the cities where their institutions were located. Others remained in the same state but moved to another city. Few headed for the sun belt to spend their retirement years.

An exception to this trend is a group of retired presidents of independent colleges and universities. About one in four of them relocated in some other region of the nation. Their reasons were not obvious. Perhaps they moved because their colleges were church-related and presidents who are members of the clergy can retire at homes provided by their religious denominations.

This tendency of former presidents to remain close to where they served as presidents invites further speculation. Perhaps they are reluctant to give up the public recognition and adulation that often accompanies a presidency. Describing his prominence in the community, one former president wrote:

There is no point in dodging the obvious. I enjoyed the prestige, the honors, the power, the recognition, and the applause of office. There are amenities and social events and privileges and opportunities and open doors because you are president. It is a heady business, even with its headaches. You are somebody, even if it is at Drooling Fangs Junior College rather than Harvard. No matter how big or how little the pond, you are the big frog.

But there is another reason why retired presidents tend to keep community ties. As the next section illustrates, retirement activities are often merely a continuation of presidential involvements.

Retirement Activities

In an earlier chapter, data on retirement activities of college and university presidents were presented. They suggest that many former academic executives devote time to college and community activities and thus maintain not only their physical presence in the community, but their professional status as well. Not surprisingly, a frequent postpresidential job is fund raising. One retired state college president wrote:

I work part-time raising money for our endowment fund. I initiated the fund while I was president and wish to see it grow. I made most of the contacts which have resulted in more than a million dollars in our fund.

Other retired presidents mentioned their work with alumni and with campus advancement activities. Of course, in the private sector some emeritus presidents are given seats on the board of trustees or are named chancellors. Some contribute to their institutions by writing a college history, and others share their experience with other academic institutions through consulting.

Civic leaders often see retired presidents as a valuable resource. Many in the survey were named to public boards. One president, for example, chaired a mayor's committee on government efficiency, and another headed the local economic development council. Directing a local museum proved to be a useful and satisfying retirement job for another retired president. The community involvement of many veteran presidents is illustrated by this response from a former community college president:

> *In retirement I am most content. I spend considerable time in community volunteer work. I chair two foundations, one a retirement program for the elderly and the other which identifies capable students who need financial assistance in college. In addition, I serve on the boards of two historical societies, have been president of Rotary, and will be governor of our Rotary district.*

Other retired presidents heed other calls. One served as president of a public urban college for two years in the mid-1960s and later entered the religious life. More than a decade later, at seventy-eight years of age, he was ordained a priest.

Some retired presidents fill their days with personal and family matters. A 92-year-old emeritus president of a small private college said:

> *I still read from great literature in Greek, Latin, English, and American. I do proofreading for a monthly consumers' newsletter, and I have a lot of correspondence with "my tribe"—six children, eleven grandchildren, two great-grandchildren, and a lot of in-laws.*

His closing salutation brought me a smile at the end of a long day of reading some rather dry responses from other former presidents. He wrote: "May God bless you in good Christian work in a state university, Dr. Robert F. Carbone."

Another retired president who was equally entertaining typed four single-spaced pages telling of his boyhood on a farm near the small western college where he served as a faculty member and president. He talked of hunting ducks with a nephew, mowing his lawn with an old-fashioned push-mower ("a six-mile walk"), and caring for his invalid wife. Recognizing that he may have been a bit garrulous, he acknowledged:

This is rather too much, but these prospective presidents should bear in mind that retirement does not necessarily mean playing golf and toying with a half dozen hobbies. I watch television, too, of course, especially the athletic contests. No soap yet, but I may get to it.

Like the above was a comment from a former president who managed to fill his days with interesting but not necessarily taxing activities. He wrote:

First let me tell you what I am not doing. I am not employed in another job. I am not consulting or advising. As I tell everyone who asks me, if I had intended to continue working, I would not have retired. What I am doing is just what I want to do, and I am so busy that I wonder how I ever found time to work. To enumerate my various activities would be to name almost everything one can do indoors or outdoors, except maybe the "make-do" hobbies one is supposed to do when he retires.

How presidents make the transition from work to a more leisurely life is the next question.

Adjustment to Retirement

Throughout this chapter are comments testifying to the adjustment former presidents make to their new way of life. Almost without exception, those surveyed responded with upbeat reports. They seemed content, involved, and eager to communicate. Of course, those who did not return the questionnaire may have had a different story to tell but, from available evidence, the trend seems positive. Typical of the responses was one from a man who had been teacher, admissions officer, dean, vice president, and president of a church-related college. In all, he devoted thirty-five years of his life to the institution, the last seventeen as its president. He admitted:

I am enjoying my retirement. I now can do what I want to do when I want to do it. I was an ordained minister . . . and am now involved in church work in a voluntary status. I am free to travel, do conference speaking, or consulting work as I want to without any pressure.

His carefree point of view was expressed by the comments of another retired president who stated:

Having been tied to a schedule very closely for many years, I've found that now I don't know what day it is, don't know what time it is, and I don't care.

Recalling the Highlights

Asking these retired college and university presidents to reflect a bit on high points in their presidential careers yielded some extremely interesting results. One trend was perplexing—very few of the group claimed to have had memorable experiences. Maybe it was false modesty. Or, perhaps it was difficulty in choosing. "All my experiences were memorable," claimed one retired president—no single experience stood out.

Among the more interesting responses were four that pointed out strikingly different events. One involved building a college, another saving a college, a third winning over the faculty, and a fourth graduating a student. Together, these reminiscences teach us something about the diverse nature of the president's role.

The highlight of one retired community college president's career was the opportunity he had to "convert a golf course into a college." He explained:

I was given a piece of paper with a directive—make this golf course into a college. [I] hired an administrative staff and faculty, negotiated the first union contract, watched development of the curriculum and student body, established resident arts groups, developed an outstanding noncredit program, produced TV programs, counseled faculty and students as needed, dedicated our new campus, and presided at the first college commencement.

For a retired president of a private college, the highlight of his presidential career derived from campus fiscal problems. He related it this way:

The greatest experience was taking a financially troubled institution, turning it around into a stable college, debt free and valued at more than seven times the original worth. With that change, it became academically stable, too.

Faculty support headed the list of memorable events in the career of a man who once administered a private university, who worked his way up the academic ladder from department head to dean, provost and, finally, president. He mentioned a successful fund drive and the acquisition of more land, but his principal memory was of "a generous official resolution of approval voted by the faculty in support of my appointment as president."

The last comment in this section will surely loom paramount in the series, especially to those who consider student development the primary mission of higher education. The retired president of a western community college shared one of his most memorable experiences with these words:

I recall granting a high school completion certificate to a 76-year-old man who responded, "With this I will be a big shot down at the Senior Citizen Center."

Thus ends the commentary from presidents who have presided over their last commencement and who no longer need to ask the parliamentarian about which substitute motion takes precedence at a faculty meeting. Those who realize the tensions and drain of presidential life will surely not deny that these veteran administrators deserve the peace and freedom that retirement seems to bring.

Their comments were, in the main, quite positive. Absent were complaints of few rewards and many pressures that flavored the remarks of their younger counterparts. Perhaps memory favors happy days; perhaps restful years have softened the blows. More likely, however, the contentment stems from something else: as one former president, quoted earlier in this book, said, "[The presidency] was the most exciting, demanding, and satisyfing experience of my life." In the job recollections of former presidents, the problems pale beside the gratifications.

PART III
LEARNING FROM THE PAST

The institution was encountering the now familiar trends of the late sixties—the Vietnam syndrome, student drug problems, capital indebtedness, a discontented and aging faculty heavily loaded with full professors at top salaries, a hostile alumni and community, a divided board, and an endowment that hadn't grown much since the Great Depression. Looking back on it, I have wondered how an individual's ego—even when his advocates have convinced him he is a potential savior descending from the feathery light of a Renaissance painting—can be so massive as to take on such an abomination. I did.
A president now in office

According to conventional wisdom, experience is a good teacher. If that is true, then people with extensive experience ought to be excellent instructors. What can be learned from the experiences of veteran college and university presidents? The last part of this book offers some answers.

In addition to documenting the postpresidential activities of a generation of academic executives, my students and I elicited from them comments about the presidency that may be of value to their successors. While in office, presidents must often temper their remarks in the interest of good internal and external relations. Once out of office, however, they are free to offer candid advice. Many of those who responded to our surveys did so, and their comments highlight the next chapter.

Presidential experience helped fashion this part of the book in a second way. In addition to asking about the current activities of many former college and university presidents, we probed their pasts and, in so doing, prompted them to share with us some of their presidential experiences. It was inevitable that this process would suggest some generalizations of interest to all who are affected (directly or indirectly) by a college presidency. In Chapter 8, these generalizations are contrasted with misguided notions about the presidency.

PART III: LEARNING FROM THE PAST

SEVEN

Straight from the Shoulder
Advice from Former College and University Presidents

Frankly, I do not know why a person would aspire to become a college or university president. There was a time when the presidency was a position of high honor and station. This has eroded, and the presidency is now a tough assignment.
Former president of a 200-year-old, church-related college

The advice with which former college and university presidents responded to this survey can be grouped into two categories: (1) the process of becoming a president (beginning to think about becoming a president, identifying role models, preparing for the task, and taking overt action toward that end); and (2) the job itself and what it takes to be a successful president. Both categories will be illustrated with the actual words of former presidents. We will begin with the process leading up to appointment as president.

Entertaining Thoughts about a Presidency

To every prospective college or university president comes a time when the thought of taking on that leadership role first occurs. The fact that it occurred early in the academic careers of some survey respondents is surprising and in sharp contrast to the conventional wisdom that says, "Wait and it will come to you—don't aspire." The former president of one private liberal arts college confessed that he

69

began thinking about becoming a president when he was an undergraduate. Another former president from the private sector also entertained such notions early in his career. He wrote:

When I was a graduate teaching assistant, I believed that there were better ways to run an institution of higher education than those used in the institution with which I was associated.

It was an administrative role, and not necessarily the presidency, that intrigued the former president of a highly regarded private university. He commented:

Academic administration was in my mind when I first became involved in a university, as a student and then as a member of the faculty, and as I worked up the administrative positions, first as a research project director, an associate dean, and as a department chairman. By the time I became president, I was pretty familiar with the problems of running a university.

Contrary to the above, some former presidents said that their first thoughts of one day assuming institutional leadership emerged only when the opportunity of appointment presented itself. The former president of a leading college of art reported:

I never thought about becoming a college president until I was asked to accept that position at the college. As a young instructor in the art department of a state college, my hope was someday to become the chairman of a good small art department in a liberal arts college. I never achieved that ambition. The [presidential] offer interested me because I knew and admired the college, because it offered me the opportunity to return to education after many years in the art museum field, and because the salary offered was a great deal more than I was getting.

Presidential thoughts were literally thrust on a man who once held and is now retired from a major public university presidency. He said:

It was never an ambition. In fact, I never gave it a thought until my predecessor was abruptly fired. I had held major administrative jobs in the nonprofit sector and in government, both of which were helpful in my presidential role.

The vast majority of former presidents, however, were neither too young nor too well seasoned when thoughts of a presidency arose. Their responses indicate that the idea of one day becoming president gradually developed as they moved up the administrative hierarchy and began to take on important responsibilities and to crystallize their views about institutional structure and management. Implicit in their comments was advice that became more explicit in responses to later questions. They counseled: there are many rungs on the career ladder, and as lesser dreams become reality, larger dreams are certain to emerge in time.

Finding Someone to Help

In the academic world, many individuals play the role of mentor. A college teacher, a dissertation advisor, an outstanding scholar, a senior department colleague are all examples. That being the case, it is surprising how few of the former presidents surveyed acknowledged the existence of an administrative mentor who assisted them in attaining a presidency. Of course, some respondents spoke warmly of teachers, colleagues, and other presidents who had helped, but a great many simply said, "I had no mentor."

Normally, mentors play an important role in all professions and vocations. They introduce neophytes to social and professional values, and they serve as role models. More importantly, they can facilitate an individual's professional advancement. If the mentor-novice relationship is healthy, it tends to dissolve gradually as the novice becomes established and gains recognition on his or her own merits. Perhaps this dissolution of the relationship explains why mentors were seldom mentioned by the college and university presidents surveyed.

Among those who did write about mentors was the former president of a private university who said:

For about two years before I left to assume a presidency, I worked rather closely with the president of my former institution. This experience provided an opportunity to observe and gain some understanding of the broad range of matters with which the president of a university must deal.

Another person, the former head of a public university, gave further testimony about the value of a mentor. He wrote:

Two individuals could be regarded as mentors. The first was a colleague ... who accepted the presidency of a major state university. My career paralleled his in a number of ways, and he served somewhat as a model. The other was president of the university where I was academic vice president. I was appointed to replace him after one and one-half years. During that time he was extremely helpful in many ways in preparing me to take his place.

Because evidence in the responses regarding the mentor's influence on a president was so diverse, it is difficult to extract one dominant piece of advice. However, the importance of having good role models was mentioned often enough to warrant such counsel. Even if a formal relationship with some senior administrator cannot be established, it is wise to identify one or more successful administrators who may be observed and whose endorsements may be solicited.

The prospective president who attempts to go it alone has a role model who is not likely to teach him very much.

Preparing for the Job

How does one prepare for the college or university presidency? Advice on this point offered by former presidents ranged from specific to general, from humorous to serious. Before turning to serious thoughts, one former president kidded:

As a preliminary I would suggest the person consult at once with a qualified mental health staff and then take a long vacation in the Caribbean.

His serious advice, which echoed that of many of his counterparts, can be summed up succinctly: If you want to be a president, there are some things you can and should do.

Repeatedly, former presidents stressed the importance of doing well in the jobs leading up to the appointment. "Be good at the thing you are doing," is the way one put it. Another said, "Consciously discharge the responsibilities which are assigned to you, whatever the nature of those responsibilities."

A third added:

Never see "becoming a president" to be as important as meeting the demands of your current job. And—in spite of military advice to the contrary—always volunteer. It is in voluntary, quasiadministrative roles of great variety that one really learns.

A second important preparation for presidential leadership mentioned by many respondents was solid faculty experience. At least ten years of teaching was prescribed by one, but most merely suggested, "Be a successful faculty member" or "Acquire academic respectability." One commented:

Get a solid academic reputation first, so that a faculty cannot dismiss you as one who does not know what it is to be a teacher-scholar.

On the other hand, faculty experience alone may not be sufficient. One respondent opined that although future presidents should have a foundation of successful teaching,

It is unlikely that one can move directly from a teaching role to the presidency unless the teaching experience has been publicly and professionally prestigious.

Several of his colleagues concurred.

Beyond classroom experience, according to many former presidents, there are other preparations aspiring presidents should make. Obtaining "command experience" was the somewhat martial requirement one retired president described. Experience in administration ("try at least two different levels," advised one respondent) is an important step. "Serve as an administrative assistant early in your career," counseled another retired president. The value of an administrative apprenticeship was stressed in many responses, and one writer even suggested:

[Future presidents should] be required to undergo two- to four-year programs of apprenticeship with a good president at a good institution—but not one where he/she plans to work.

A few respondents were surprisingly specific in their advice about how to prepare for the presidency. "Business administration and human understanding" were the key factors suggested by one respondent; another said a "business and legal background" was important; a third argued for "philosophy of education and business management." Only one former president out of the hundreds who replied asserted that a doctorate in management or administration was a vital prerequisite to the presidency.

Consistent with the latter point was the dearth of evidence in the survey that the respondents had selected their graduate programs with a presidential career in mind. Only two former presidents, both of whom had administered community colleges, revealed that they had done so. One wrote: "I undertook studies which were designed to provide me with the administrative knowledge needed to assume a presidency."

His colleague concurred:

My first serious thoughts about becoming a president developed when I was about half way "up the ladder." One positive conscious step was to pursue education designed to contribute to my knowledge of performing the task, as opposed to pursuing an educational route simply intended to culminate in an illustrious degree.

The highly respected former head of a land-grant university summed up much of the advice about preparing for a presidency with these insights:

First, become a dedicated scholar in your own field and put forth special effort in helping determine directions for your own academic department. Assume extra responsibility at the college and institutional level so as better to get acquainted with problems and policy matters at all levels of the university. This will usually be through committee assignments. Seek out some kind of administrative apprenticeship, either in your own university or another.

Voicing Presidential Aspirations

Evidence suggests that some of these individuals entertained thoughts of the presidency early in their careers. Some even took overt action. The advice most former college and university presidents gave, however, was to the contrary: Keep your thoughts and actions to yourself. Some cautioned against even indulging in such aspirations. "Don't campaign for the job," said one former president, who was supported by another who declared:

It is too narrow an aspiration to have. Instead, I would suggest that the individual aspire to exerting educational leadership—whether it be as a chairman, dean, vice president, or faculty member. If these activities are enjoyable and are done well, other opportunities will come.

The words of one emeritus president of a public university were even stronger:

At no time prior to the opening of a presidential position should you voice active interest in becoming president. The position should seek the man, and the man should not seek the position.

Two former presidents, also from the public sector, suggested that aspiring too boldly to a presidency often foretells failure. Having served as president of two major state universities, as well as dean and vice president in two others, one respondent observed:

I can say that most of the people I have known over the years who seemed to plainly want and overtly seek such a position were rather precisely the kinds of individuals who were lacking in those very characteristics that solid performance in such a position calls for.

The other former president said:

My observation has been that those who single-mindedly and openly aspire to becoming university presidents are less likely than others to succeed.

From all the comments emerged a consensus: Successful presidential careers are built one step at a time. A gradual unfolding of leadership opportunities and a gradual honing of leadership skills are essential to success as a college or university president.

General Words of Advice

The survey elicited a wealth of advice on the job of president and the personal traits of successful college and university presidents. To be sure, some expresidents were a bit flip in their responses. One said, "Avoid periods like 1968-71," and another advised "doing away with search committees." However, the serious comments seemed to suggest two broad themes: demands of the job and the personal characteristics of presidents.

76   LEARNING FROM THE PAST

The first theme was introduced by the former president who averred that "the job of being president is much more difficult and less rewarding than you think."

A partial explanation for this observation was provided by a colleague who advised presidents:

Protect your time, know your stress limits, be prepared to spend inordinate amounts of time on ceremony, trivia, and meatloaf.

The feeling was more soberly expressed by one whose post-presidential activities included directing an organization devoted to assisting presidents. He wrote:

Be prepared for demands on your time and that of your family that extend beyond regular hours of work. Be prepared to spend an inordinate amount of time keeping trustees informed and prepared for changes that are coming. Adopt as a vital part of your administrative style the long-range planning process, and involve all of your constituencies. Always maintain in clear focus the purpose of your institution and communicate that purpose to others.

Four additional comments reveal a second theme: the personal qualities central to presidential success. Having headed a private college for some years, one former president counseled:

Be flexible, tough-skinned, have good control of your ego, and understand that you will never make a "right" decision in the eyes of at least a part of your public and employees.

A somewhat lighter note was struck by a colleague who advised:

Don't take yourself too seriously. Keep your sense of humor. Recognize you are not infallible, and don't expect to be. When you make an error, admit it.

The former president of a community college spelled out an extensive list of personal characteristics for presidents:

Be a humanist in heart, soul, and mind. Be absolutely reliable, for it is your responsibility to set the tone for the institution. Eliminate the words "I" and "my" from your vocabulary; substitute "What do you think?" "Is it possible?" and "Do you suppose we can?" Your job is to provide opportunities for other people to develop their potential to the fullest—keep out of their way. Pray for humility. Study hard, work hard, play hard, keep your nose clean, and stroke your imagination. Remember, you are always walking a tight rope high in the air. Sometimes it gets awfully windy up there. Hang on to your balance.

Finally, the following words were offered by the son of a homestead farmer who began teaching in a small North Dakota town after one year of college and subsequently returned to his college to become president. Despite his humble background, he has words to offer that should be heeded by presidents in any station in life.

Be scrupulously honest, fair, reasonable, and decent. Don't be a pompous stuffed shirt. Have your coffee with the janitors or the students once in a while. Remember that you can get a lot done if you don't care who gets the credit. And, for heaven's sake, know what you are talking about when you present your budget.

PART III: LEARNING FROM THE PAST

EIGHT

Illusions about Presidential Leadership
Myths and Realities about Presidents and the Presidency

Today the president is pretty much a "clerk of the works." He keeps track of government regulations, union negotiations, computer printouts, and whose ox is about to be gored. He doesn't need to have an idea in his head or the gumption to make a decision because that is all taken care of by one of a host of committees. If nothing ever gets done, there is no one to blame because the president is far out of sight behind all those committees. By the same token, he doesn't get credit either for any "good" things that might happen. There is no joy in that!
Retired president of a state college

Often, the final chapter of a book is devoted to summarizing all that has gone before. Not so here. This chapter serves a larger purpose.

My study of the presidency led me through several interesting activities—more than two decades of president watching, reading books and articles on the subject, discussing ideas with many others interested in this topic, conducting a survey of institutions, teaching a seminar on the presidency, and completing a series of follow-up studies. What has been reported up to this point stems chiefly from the institutional survey and the follow-up studies. This chapter integrates those data with generalizations about presidents and the presidency gleaned from the full range of activities in this study. What emerges is a set of realities that should dispel prevailing myths about college and university presidents and about the office of president in American higher education.

If this book generates any controversy (or even any strong feelings), no doubt the pages that follow will be the cause. My purpose in posing diametrically opposite assertions in the form of myths and realities is to raise hackles and stimulate debate. This technique is entirely my own device and cannot be blamed on my students, on the presidents who responded to our inquiries, or on others who have written about the presidency.

Onward.

Myth: *A presidency is a presidency is a presidency.*

Too much of what is said and written about college and university presidents—including much of this book—seems to suggest that there is some singular, definable office called a presidency. All too often it is convenient to generalize about this office as if the demands it makes on incumbents were everywhere the same. Of course, that is not the case at all.

Reality: *The job of president differs widely from campus to campus and, in large measure, is defined by the size, type, tradition, and control of each institution.*

In this country, institutions of higher education that enroll a few hundred students have presidents just as do higher education systems that serve more than a hundred thousand students. Some of these institutions have one principal goal while others have multiple missions. Civil authority controls some while sectarian precepts dominate others. Further, it hardly need be said that the "council of presidents," even of an association that purports to represent similar institutions, is rarely if ever a "council of equals." Thus, statements about "the presidency" must be made cautiously or, at least, clarify just what kind of presidency is being discussed.

(Having delivered myself of this admonition, I will proceed to violate it in the rest of this chapter.) □

Myth: *The president's job is clearly defined and understood by those it touches.*

Just as we may think there is *a* presidency, we often think there is a commonly accepted role for presidents to play. Perhaps reading announcements of presidential vacancies helps fuel this misconception, for the ads all sound the same. The problem is, the people who write ads are not those who finally select presidents. Worse yet, the perceptions of ad writers and interviewers differ considerably from the perceptions of interviewees. Furthermore, an institution's faculty members are sure to have yet another view of what their president should do. As in all mortal affairs, the seeds of confusion can sprout easily in a fertile environment of conflicting expectations.

Reality: *The president's job is what each president makes it.*

Regardless of advertisements, position descriptions, or letters of appointment (few presidents sign contracts), it is up to each president to develop a style and define a span of control that will characterize his or her administration. Inevitably this will happen, whether by design or by accident. There have been presidents who never turned out a light or opened a letter because, as one told me once, "If I do that, I am not thinking about the things I should be thinking about!" On the other hand, there have been presidents who inspected classroom chairs to determine which should be repaired and which discarded. Clearly, concepts of presidential leadership vary widely. □

Myth: *Presidents have a plan of action and provide leadership for their institutions.*

When a new president arrives on campus, people often assume that tucked somewhere in his or her mind is a grand design for moving the institution ahead. Too often, however, the new president knows little about the institution because the search process, by its very nature, does not facilitate an even exchange of information. Furthermore, the new president usually has no time to form any comprehensive plan because being interviewed (maybe at more than one place), clearing up business back home, selling the house, and moving the family just doesn't leave time for such planning. Moreover, the conservative nature of academe has taught most aspiring presidents the difference between holding the tiller and making waves.

Reality: *Few presidents are proactive; most react to circumstances and pressures.*

There may have been a day, in the dim and distant past, when colleges and universities were isolated and removed from the mainstream of society. (What else explains the notion of closeted scholars and ivory towers?) Today, that has changed. Presidents now deal with many constituencies, most of whom are informed, organized, and aware of the power they can wield. Public sector presidents now answer to private sources of support (and pressure) while private college heads have had to pay more attention to state and federal agencies as their public subsidies increase. The erosion of institutional autonomy, resulting from legislative action, bureaucratic regulation, and superboard policy, is nowhere more clearly revealed than in the decreasing ability of presidents to exert clear, decisive leadership. If presidents lead today, they do so not by dint of title or station but because they have better data, unflagging energy, keen political instincts, and the patience to measure progress in inches rather than miles. □

Myth: *Presidents are in charge of their institutions.*

The histories of many institutions tell of some early-day president who hired, fired, promoted, did the budget, and taught a course or two each term to boot. When institutions were small and times less complicated, it may have been possible for presidents to play that role. Today, however, presidents of even the smallest institutions can do little more than keep informed about happenings on campus. The internal management gap has been filled by a battalion of subordinate administrative officers who field the problems, work out accommodations, and generally keep the shop running. As the range of problems increases, so does the cadre of middle managers and the cost of administering the institution. Increasing costs, as well as the proliferation of middle managers, disturb faculty members who tend to think there is a high, positive correlation between the time a president spends on campus and his effectiveness.

Reality: *Presidents are external agents.*

In professional football, wide receivers score points, and so it is with presidents. They must stay on the edge of academic lineplay to deal with the many constituencies on whom their institutions depend. Once, they were concerned with only the board, a few alumni, and the biennial legislative session (public college presidents only). But times have changed, and so have the presidents. The community, state, and national scene command most presidential attention today, and those presidents who play well on that stage tend to accomplish the most for their institutions. ☐

Myth: *Boards make policy; presidents administer it.*

In the best of all possible worlds, as Dr. Pangloss would say, enlightened governing boards set clear policy directions and then permit the institution's chief administrative officer to carry out their intent. But, of course, such textbook cases seldom occur in real life. Board members, if strongly committed (or sorely misguided), often infringe on administrative territory. Presidents, if they are decisive, often formulate policy in the act of decision making. Boards that dominate their presidents often stifle creative administration. Presidents who dominate their boards often get too far out on the limb. In either situation, the institution suffers.

Reality: *Policy is usually vague, and a board often does not understand its role.*

Those who come to academe searching for clear, finely tuned policy manuals are usually disappointed. The tradition in many places was never to write anything down. This tactic preserved maximum flexibility in dealing with problems and pleased both faculty and administrators. (The students, unfortunately, usually got the short end of the stick.) Codification of institutional policy has emerged of necessity in recent times, but some will argue that merely putting policy in a book has not improved things that much. Furthermore, when it comes to making policy, governing boards have no special qualifications. In the private sector they are selected, in most cases, because of their potential for giving or raising money, while their public sector counterparts, if not elected, have political connections. Educating the board without appearing to is an important task that any president must do and do well. To neglect it is to court trouble. ☐

Myth: *Shared governance prevents a president from exercising authority.*

The diffusion of decision making throughout the academic structure has often been blamed as the cause for some presidential and institutional failures. Although it cannot be denied that academic authority has, in large measure, been delegated to departments, colleges, and faculty committees, it is more likely that the reasons for presidential inaction and institutional inertia lie elsewhere.

Reality: *Presidents have power, and some presidents know how to use it.*

The key to understanding why some presidents are effective, aggressive leaders while others are not is in *delegation*. Virtually every institution of higher education has only one legal or traditional seat of authority—the governing board. This authority and the power that accompanies it are normally delegated to the president and by him or her to the faculty. But the ultimate responsibility for action remains with the executive officer. When faculties exercise authority effectively, presidents can act. When faculties are slow, timid, or misguided in their exercise of authority, presidents can still act, but many don't. The creative use of power in stimulating faculty action or in moving ahead despite a lack of faculty support is a quality that separates effective presidents from those who merely occupy the office. □

Myth: *Presidents have impact.*

The great colleges and universities of America were built by strong presidents who lived at a time when their sheer strength could deliver not only academic respectability but also libraries, laboratories, and classrooms. Today, the opportunities for such personal and institutional greatness are scarce if existent at all. Now the costs are astronomical, the governance and coordination structure smothering, and the demographics depressing.

Reality: *Few presidents leave their mark.*

It is doubtful whether there will be any more of those larger-than-life college and university presidents extolled in the books of education historians. Building institutional greatness is what made them giants in their times. Unfortunately, the great colleges and universities of America have probably been built already. Worse yet, the 1980s were born in a kind of breach delivery that will make institutional greatness even harder to achieve today. This is not to say, however, that institutions cannot improve, even in the worst of times. Some will improve and, as a result, some modern-day presidents will gain a measure of fame for their work. Perhaps it would be wise for presidents now in office and those who will succeed them to set for themselves more modest and attainable goals. □

Myth: *The president's "team" works together to support his or her efforts.*

It is generally assumed that a president surrounds himself or herself with subordinates who are committed to one set of goals and who are eager to move the institution in that direction. Unfortunately, that is not always the case. Presidents often inherit most of their staff members and must attempt to forge a working team out of them. Because subordinate officers rarely play a major role in presidential selection, few of them know much about their new leader. Many carve out their own piece of the action and hold on to it. (There have been stories, for example, about financial vice presidents who tell the president as little as possible about the budget.) Therefore, the importance of building an effective presidential staff is hard to overstate.

Reality: *Presidential staffs are not always carefully built.*

Two factors mitigate against a president having the kind of staff support so vital to success. First, being reluctant to disrupt too many administrative careers and thus generate unnecessary staff antipathy, new presidents try to reassign personnel they inherit in an effort to create a workable staff structure. At best, they may bring in one or two new staff members to fill key positions. Second, most academics have not had extensive experience in building and working with administrative staffs. Many new presidents face for the first time in their careers the task of organizing a large administrative team—a challenge quite different from managing the affairs of an academic department or coordinating the work of department heads. □

Myth: *The president's spouse is a vital part of the team.*

Many of the books and articles on presidential selection insist that the candidate's spouse (usually meaning wife) should be interviewed with the candidate. Historically, the spouse has played an important part in any presidential career: witness the considerable list of books on the topic. The traditional concept of a presidential wife is one of a long-suffering good hostess who always smiles and is able to tolerate long periods of time without seeing her husband. She was expected to sacrifice all her personal and professional aspirations to those of her husband. Now things are changing.

Reality: *Presidential spouses may be playing new roles.*

Several factors appear to be changing the role of spouses. First, because more women are being appointed to presidencies, the president's spouse may now be a husband and not a wife. Men need not (maybe, dare not) subordinate their careers to that of a wife who climbs the administrative ladder. Second, there are more and more presidents who have no spouse. Finally, many presidential wives, educated and talented women, have developed career directions of their own; such factors limit their role as spouse of the president. Perhaps, then, it is time for an addition to the literature on presidential spouses that addresses the two-career presidential mansion. □

Myth: *The job seeks the person.*

This notion, so deeply ingrained in the academic mind, will be hard to refute. Yet there is considerable evidence to the contrary. Some presidents admit that they not only sought the job but prepared for it. Foundations, consulting firms, and higher education graduate programs often see themselves as president makers, actively trying to position the right person in the right place at the right time. Affirmative action has resulted in widespread recruiting that turns up long lists of eager candidates, many of whom would never have been sought by "the job." The truth is that many who actively seek presidencies get selected and, once in office, appear to be as effective as their more coy brethren.

Reality: *It is all right to aspire to be president—but do it with a little class.*

Given current conditions, keeping presidential aspirations entirely submerged may be a handicap. It is wise to confide this goal to someone who knows the academic ropes and can help put the goal in perspective. A mentor, by any name, is a valuable asset to any young academic who is secretly entertaining thoughts of a presidency. A mentor can help provide valuable experiences that can make scholarly credentials even more appealing, and suggest ways of molding an academic career so that when "the job" goes out "seeking," the aspirant will not be too hard to find. Such tactics should prove especially effective today, when large, diverse search committees must plow through the credentials of hundreds of candidates. It is also important to keep in mind that despite affirmative action, search committees, and nationwide recruiting, many presidential searches are not entirely open, and governing boards do not always appoint the most qualified person. □

Myth: *Old presidents return to teaching.*

Much of the testimony in this book counters this notion.

Reality: *Most presidents who leave office enjoy active professional lives in the nonacademic world.*

According to the survey, although the college or university presidency highlighted many a career, it was not the grand finale. After the presidency comes an opportunity to engage in activities that are certainly interesting, usually less taxing, often more enjoyable and, in most cases, more lucrative. The array of positions that ex-presidents assume is impressive and, generally, these persons give enthusiastic reports about their activities. Not only is there life after the presidency but, in unknown ways, the college or university presidency trains individuals for a wide variety of interesting activities outside academe. □

Myth: *The presidency is "splendid agony."*

Given all that this book has revealed about the presidency, the true nature of the job emerges—

Reality: *The presidency is "splendid agony."* □

POSTSCRIPT
SPLENDID AGONY REVISITED

Candid recollections and postpresidential activities of a generation of former presidents provided the substance for this analysis of the American college and university presidency. These pages, it is hoped, offer new insights into the office and the men and women who fill it.

If presidents do not appear larger than life in this book, neither is their contribution to education progress downgraded. Their comments about academic leadership reveal examples of presidential verve and languor, executive flair and stuffiness, far-ranging vision and pettifoggery.

If the presidency is not excessively glorified in these pages, neither has it been unduly tarnished. Looking back on their years as education leaders, these former presidents confirm that the office they once held offers burdens as well as blessings, pleasure along with pain, frustration in addition to challenge.

Given this conflicting picture, the term "splendid agony" (an oxymoron according to my editor) provides a meaningful if somewhat melodramatic context for understanding presidents, the presidency, and the career passages that presidents make.

Looking back often suggests what may lie ahead, and recounting the journeys of others may help those newly come to the road see more clearly where they are going. Future generations of college and university presidents, then, should think seriously about what lies ahead and plan their routes carefully.

Suggestions For Further Reading

Anderson, B. Robert. "The Willing Masochist," *The Philadelphia Inquirer*, 13 May 1973, pp. 30-32.

Anon. "How Long can a President Serve Effectively?" *College Management*, November 1971, p. 26.

Atwell, Charles A. "The Independent Junior College President: Profiles and Career Patterns," *Community College Frontiers*, Winter 1980, pp. 38-42.

Bennis, Warren G. *The Leaning Ivory Tower*. San Francisco: Jossey-Bass, 1975.

Buxton, T. H., et al. "University Presidents: Academic Chameleons," *Educational Record*, Spring 1976, pp. 79-86.

Callcott, George H., Ed. *Forty Years as a College President: Memoirs of Wilson Elkins*. College Park: University of Maryland, 1981.

Carmichael, John H. "Origin and Mobility of Presidents," *Junior College Journal*, May 1969, pp. 30-32.

Cohen, Michael D. and James G. March. *Leadership and Ambiguity: The American College President*. New York: McGraw-Hill, 1974.

Cole, Charles C., Jr. "The Reeling Presidency," *Educational Record*, Spring 1976, pp. 71-78.

Corbally, Marguerite Walker. *The Partners: Sharing the Life of a College President*. Danville, Ill.: Interstate Printers and Publishers, 1977.

Cowley, W. H. *Presidents, Professors, and Trustees*. San Francisco: Jossey-Bass, 1980.

Demerath, Nicholas H., Richard W. Stephens, and Robb R. Taylor. *Power, Presidents, and Professors*. New York: Basic Books, 1967.

Dodds, H. W. *The Academic President: Educator or Caretaker*. New York: McGraw-Hill, 1962.

Eells, W. C. and E. V. Hollis. *The College Presidency 1900-1960: An Annotated Bibliography*. Washington, D.C.: U.S. Office of Education, 1961.

Eells, Walter C. "The College President's Wife," *Liberal Education*, October 1961, pp. 358-404.

Ferrari, Michael R. *Profiles of American College Presidents*. East Lansing: Michigan State University Business Studies, 1970.

Horn, Francis H. "The Job of the President," *Liberal Education*, October 1969, pp. 387-92.

Hutchins, R. *No Friendly Voice*. Baton Rouge: Louisiana State University Press, 1936.

Jones, Thomas E., Edward V. Stanford, and Goodrich C. White. *Letter to College Presidents*. Englewood Cliffs, N.J.: Prentice-Hall, 1964.

Kauffman, Joseph F. *At the Pleasure of the Board: The Service of the College and University President*. Washington, D.C.: American Council on Education, 1980.

———. "The New College President: Expectations and Realities," *Educational Record*, Spring 1977, pp. 146-68.

Kintzer, Ruth. *The President's Wife: A Handbook for Wives of New Community College Presidents*. Santa Monica, Cal.: Pine Publications, 1972.

Kleinpell, E. H. *In the Shadow: Reflections of a State College President*. River Falls, Wisconsin: University of Wisconsin Press, 1975.

Knox, Warren Barr. *Eye of the Hurricane: Observation on Creative Educational Administration*. Corvallis: Oregon State University Press, 1973.

Lindahl, Charles W. "Attrition of College Administrators," *Intellect*, February 1973, pp. 289-93.

Lowell, A. L. *What a University President Has Learned*. New York: Macmillan, 1938.

Mayhew, Lewis B. and James R. Glenn, Jr. "College and University Presidents: Roles in Transition," *Liberal Education*, October 1975, pp. 299-308.

McKenna, David L. "Recycling College Presidents," *Liberal Education*, December 1972, pp. 456-63.

Suggestions for Further Reading 91

Ness, Frederic W. *An Uncertain Glory*. San Francisco: Jossey-Bass, 1971.

Prator, Ralph. *The College President*. Washington, D.C.: The Center for Applied Research in Education, 1963.

Pray, Francis C. "The President As 'Reasonable Adventurer,'" *AGB Reports*, May/June 1979, pp. 45-48.

Prichard, Keith W. *et al.* "The Problems of College and University Presidents," *School and Society*, No. 100 (1972), pp. 104-106.

Ritchie, M. A. F. *The College Presidency: Initiation into the Order of the Turtle*. New York: Philosophical Library, 1970.

———. "Emeritus, Thank God," *College and University*, April 1974, pp. 34-35.

Roueche, John E. "The Junior College President," *Junior College Research Review*, 2, No. 10 (1968).

Selden, William K. "How Long is a College President?" *Liberal Education*, March 1960, pp. 5-15.

"Special Section [on college presidents]." *Community and Junior College Journal*, October 1980, pp. 17-48.

Stoke, H. W. *The American College President*. New York: Harper and Row, 1959.

Thwing, C. F. *The College President*. New York: Macmillan, 1926.

Tunnicliffe, Guy W. and John A. Ingram. "The College President: Who Is He?" *Educational Record*, Spring 1969, pp. 189-93.

Walker, Donald E. "Goodbye, Mr. President, and Good Luck!" *Educational Record*, Winter 1977, pp. 53-58.